D1078897

Neil Forsyth is an author and journalist. A fellow Dundonian and friend to Bob Servant for over twenty years, his *Delete This At Your Peril – The Bob Servant Emails* is now available from Birlinn in a newly expanded edition. Forsyth is also author of *Other People's Money*, the biography of fraudster Elliot Castro, and a novel, *Let Them Come Through*.

Also by Neil Forsyth

Delete This at Your Peril – The Bob Servant Emails

Non Fiction

Other People's Money – The Rise and Fall of Britain's Most Audacious Fraudster (with Elliot Castro)

Fiction

Let Them Come Through

www.neilforsyth.com

Bob Servant
Hero of Dundee

Neil Forsyth

BIRLINN

First published in 2010 by
Birlinn Limited
West Newington House
10 Newington Road
Edinburgh
EH9 1QS

www.birlinn.co.uk

Reprinted 2011

ISBN: 978 1 84158 920 6

British Library Cataloguing-in-Publication Data
A catalogue record for this book is available from the British Library

Photographs on pp. xvii, 31, 52, 57, 59, 60, 61, 64, 82,
89, 93, 108, 124 © Jim Gove; photograph on p. xx
reproduced by permission of Getty Images

Typeset by Brinnoven, Livingston
Printed and bound by Cox and Wyman Ltd, Reading

For my wee sister Carol,
with love.

Contents

Introduction
by Neil Forsyth

It's a great privilege to stand sentry over another offering from Dundee's own Bob Servant and what an occasion it is. If you had suggested to me a few years ago that Bob would write his autobiography with my assistance I would have been surprised. If you'd told me a few months ago I would have been astonished for the book you hold has been a labour of love. This is not my story of course but perhaps, through my experience, you can catch an early glimpse of your companion for the next hundred or so pages. I can certainly offer a window to a fascinating mind.

I met Bob Servant twenty years ago, when I was twelve and he was a glamorous local personality. Since then we have built a friendship based on football, distrust and the bars of our shared hometown of Broughty Ferry, Dundee.

Two years ago I edited a book for Bob and it wasn't an altogether unpleasant experience. I was therefore interested when he approached me to edit his memoirs. For his many faults Bob has lived a fascinating life and he was offering to 'open cans of worms' on various matters that I felt could have a wide audience. Dundee's Cheeseburger Wars of the 1980s (in which Bob played a dominant role) are often described by social commentators as the closest a British city has come to anarchy in modern history, while I felt Bob's knowledge of local government corruption could be a damning indictment on the traditional flaws of localised political control.

Although living in America, I agreed to return to Dundee for six months and help shape Bob's memories. From there we swiftly entered the realms of disaster. It must appear churlish for an autobiography's lowly editor to open a book by denigrating the book's subject but it is hard for me to do otherwise when the horrors of the experience are so fresh in my mind. Editing a book is a demanding task at the best of times. When it is conducted against a backdrop of committed insanity it becomes truly torturous.

The initial problem was finding Bob. After greeting my arrival in Dundee with the promise of 'going at it hammer and tongs' we then began an exhausting cat and mouse existence. Ever since selling his cheeseburger van business and before that his window-cleaning enterprise for large, possibly untaxed, sums Bob has lived a life predictable only through commitment to whims and flights of fancy. Every day for weeks I'd spend long hours trying to track him down after another appointment went unmet. When I found him I'd be given an elaborate cover story backed by evident falsehood[1] and the assurance that 'tomorrow is D-Day'. I realised with horror that the only way I could get the book finished was to move into Bob's house.

I needed to move anyway. I'd been staying at my family home but Bob had effortlessly managed to strain my relationship with my parents. Bob rarely calls mobile phones because he believes they are 'a fiver a minute' so got my parents' number from the phone book and called the house directly. Unfortunately Bob enjoys beginning phone calls to associates by impersonating a police officer reporting a misdemeanour. With my parents of retirement age it was an exhausting and often traumatic experience to continually assure them I had not committed the various crimes Bob would suggest in those opening, comic stages of his calls.

With immediate regret I took up residence, and ultimately refuge, in Bob's spare room. He would wake me in the morning in a variety of ways. If he'd enjoyed a night of revelry he'd come in wearing his pyjamas, sit at the end of my bed and relate the previous evening in studied detail. Many times I would have been with Bob for the duration of the evening in question and yet he would show no hesitation in reporting an entirely different set of events to which I had witnessed. There would be exaggeration or even outright fabrication with regards

---

1 Memorably, he once swore blind that he had not (as his neighbour Frank had told me) gone to the swimming baths despite the fact that when I found him he was standing in the shallow end of the swimming baths. He told me that he was 'looking for someone' and so he hadn't actually 'gone to the swimming baths' because he was 'looking for someone' who might be there. It turned out he was secretly training to swim the River Tay, a project that followed the pattern for such things by being quietly dropped a few days later.

to the physical attraction any females had felt towards Bob, while his memory would often fail him in recounting how successful any jokes he'd made during the night had been.

On other occasions Bob would generously incorporate my bedroom into his morning grooming routine. If I was lucky, I would wake up to Bob whistling and brushing his hair into shape beside my bed. Other times I was less fortunate. I will, sadly, never lose the memory of the morning that Bob walked calmly into my bedroom wearing only a towel. He'd been in the bath when he had remembered an admittedly interesting biographical note that he thought I should have 'hot off the press'. Bob then proceeded to tell me this story while drying himself.

At first he simply lifted one foot to a chair and, side on to my nervous presence, began to dry his undercarriage with a see sawing effect. His left thigh hid the engine room of his fading build but in many ways this was worse. While he spoke energetically of an event from the early 1970s I found it hard not to imagine the effects of his coarse towelling. My imagination was soon no longer required.

In a spectacular alignment, as if matching a physical crescendo to that of the conversation, Bob coquettishly dropped his left foot to the floor. With the morning sunlight that peeked through the blinds showing as stripes across his flesh, Bob hunched and held the towel taut between his legs. I had seconds to come to terms with what was about to happen and it wasn't enough. Bob's hands set off, the towel once more began it's see-saw swing and with every flick, what he refers to with dedication as Bobby Junior bounced into the air in a small lunge towards me.

Of course now I wish (often, if not daily) that I had shown the necessary sharpness to pull my cover over my eyes. Yet half asleep and near-frozen with horror I found myself uncomfortably transfixed. I remember only how it ended. 'And that,' said Bob calmly as mayhem reigned around his midriff, 'is why you shouldn't trust a golfer.' He walked with great certainty from the room.

* * *

Compared to the towel incident, other irritations with Bob probably seem more innocent. There was his gleeful discovery of my dictaphone which was closely followed by the 'jokes' he'd leave on it for me. Sometimes he'd be a dog, sometimes he would be a child calling for help because they were 'trapped in the machine', sometimes a high-pitched woman saying she'd 'seen me on the bus' and would I like to give her 'the good stuff'?

I began to get a feel for Bob's monumental mood swings which belong on a scale all of their own. Great, victorious breakfasts could be followed by afternoons when he huddled in his armchair, muttering darkly about a perceived slight from a local shopkeeper or the postman. Bob thrives on company and reacts poorly when he lacks it. If I went to bed at what he saw as an overly early time, for example, he would wait an hour then burst into my room dressed as a 'ghost'.

The cumulative effect of all this was that I had what I am not too proud to call a minor breakdown. Two months before the book was to be delivered all Bob had achieved was to reduce me to a nervous, insomniac wreck with a phobia of the male genitals. Through the tweaking of key lifestyle choices, I could have achieved all that without leaving America.

To his credit, Bob was sufficiently shocked by my reaction to begin writing. For several weeks he worked religiously on an opus that grew around him while I watched with pride. 'Not yet,' he'd say with a wink when I tried to steal an early look at his work, followed by a range of comments regarding omelettes, eggs and, cryptically, ducks.

I therefore had at least some lingering hope when Bob finally gave me his work. Any literary ambitions I had were instantly swiped. I had developed giddy visions of working with material that could be pitched somewhere between Samuel Pepys and Charles Pooter. What I was handed belonged more fittingly between Adrian Mole and the *Beano*. Admittedly I greatly enjoyed Bob's memories with their raw fury and ambition, but then the editing process started and Bob had his final joke at my expense.

No 64-year-old man could write an autobiography that didn't stray into inaccuracy but very few would produce one that was so firmly planted in, at best, exaggeration and, at worst, libellous fantasy. I tried to omit as little as possible but even correcting what is there, as you shall see, was a substantial task.

Once I knew Bob's word was shaky I retreated to Dundee's Central Library to trawl through six decades of local newspaper archives and simultaneously make hundreds of phone calls to those Bob mentions in the book. The reaction I had from former and current associates of

Bob varied from the bewildered to the angry and, surprisingly often, to the threatening. Some of the physical forfeits people suggested I would suffer if particular content stayed in the book were incredible, particularly when you consider I was talking to pensioners and many of them were female. On this development Bob was unusually comforting, which should have raised my suspicions. I later found out he'd contacted the most ferocious of those threatening me because of what he had written and offered *them* his 'full support' in their criminal ambitions against *me*.

The day I finished this book, documented later in the Acknowledgements, was one of rare delight and I can now look upon it with some pride. I apologise for what you may see as a rant but I, selfishly, feel better for having delivered it. Anyway, I now retreat to the editorial footnotes and leave the centre stage to a man more fitted for it than me. From here on in it's just you and Bob. I can only wish you the very best of luck.

Neil Forsyth
New York
2010

A Big 'Hello' From Bob Servant

Well, well, well. Here we are again, back in the book game. I wasn't going to do another book. I'm a busy man and I have a lot of hobbies but ever since I wrote the last one I've had people asking me to write another book. Come on, Bob, they say, write another book. I try and ignore them or pass them off with bits and pieces (jokes, stories, a bit of patting) but after a while all these little jibes turn into an avalanche and the only way I can stop being buried is to stand up and shout 'Fuck's sake shut up I'll do it OK!'

After I'd decided to write another one I had to decide what type of book to write. I wasn't going to do another one of emails. I've had my fun with that stuff and it's very important as an author that I don't get pigeonholed like Dick Francis. That left a few areas but the one type of book I've always enjoyed is autobiographies. If you're a big fish and you want to write a book then the autobiography pond is the only place worth swimming. Jesus kicked it all off with the Bible and every star name since has had a crack. Wogan did it with that one where he's wearing a blazer and grinning like the cat that got the cream (which he did, to be fair, for fifty years) and from memory Savile wrote three of the bastards.[2]

Once I'd decided to write my autobiography I got the boy Forsyth in to edit. He was a pain in the arse to be honest, very lazy and a bit off in the head. I remember one day when he just totally lost it, saying how I'd ruined his life and all this. Well if giving someone a chance in life is ruining their life then it's a very strange world we live in. I suppose I shouldn't be too hard on him. What do you expect from someone who's in their forties and has never had a proper job?[3]

---

2 Bob's spot-on here. The television presenter and DJ Sir Jimmy Savile penned three autobiographies in a productive five-year burst – *As it happens* (1974), *Love is an Uphill Thing* (1976) and *God'll Fix It* (1979).
3 I'm 32.

When I sat down to write my story I started off by listing all the things I've done. It was a real eye-opener. It turned out I've done more stuff than anyone in Dundee and yet the arrogance of some of the people round here would make you sick. I looked at the list and I thought, 'I'm a hero.' Then I worried that maybe I was biased or drunk so I put my clothes back on, walked round the house and came back to the list and read it as if it was about someone else. You know what I thought? 'This guy's a hero.'

But I'm not. No-one's ever said I'm a hero and it's not because they don't want me to get a big head. It's because they don't think I am one. So I started writing and I didn't stop until I'd worked out every reason that I've not become what I should have become. It was hard to write in places, some noses are going to be put out of joint and the boo boys will have a field day.

I don't care. Because my name is Bob Servant. I should be the Hero of Dundee but it's just not happened. And here's why.

Bob Servant
Dundee
2010

Bob Servant (left) and Neil Forsyth. Broughty Ferry, Dundee, 2010

We are all born mad. Some remain so.
Samuel Beckett (1906–1989)

Show me a hero and I will write you a tragedy.
Anonymous

I don't believe in God.
Sir Terry Wogan (1938–)

Photo courtesy of Bob Servant's private collection, all rights reserved.
Inscription on back of photograph reads: 'Dawson Park, 1954'.

1

The Lone Ranger Being
a Lot of Bollocks

Until I was ten years old life for me was all about The Lone Ranger and I wish I'd never bothered. These days there are all sorts of rules with regards to kids. It's all fresh vegetables and people frowning at you if you spank them (especially if they're not yours). Well how times change, because when I was a nipper it was a complete free-for-all.

The first school I went to was Eastern Primary next to the mousetrap factory.[4] Working in the mousetrap factory made the folk there completely immersed in violence and they took it out on us. Every morning a kid would come in with a shiner or a dead leg. The headmaster went over to the factory to sort it out but the manager kicked him in the balls and after that our lesson times were switched so we didn't clash with the factory's shift changes.

It opened my eyes to violence and taught me that it could be an important weapon as long as you used it on someone that wasn't as good at it as you were. I was also scared, just a little bit, but scared enough. Even with the shift changes, you never knew when you'd bump into someone from the mousetrap factory in the streets around the school. I was lucky enough to avoid some of the hidings that others got but I picked up the odd slap and got chased home once by a woman that had just come off the nightshift.

---

4 For a forty-year period, from the 1920s to the mid 1960s, the Daly and Sons factory on Dundee's Great Eastern Road was the centre of the European mousetrap industry. The factory closed on Tuesday 3 August 1965. See *The Dundee Courier* of the same date – '*Mice Celebrate on Black Day For City*'.

It wasn't really something that I could bring up at home. Conversation was always encouraged at our house but not if I was involved. That was a pretty rigid rule which made it very hard for me to introduce topics. Every night Mum and Dad gave me a bag of chips and a glass of Barr's Limeade then sat me in front of the telly while they went off and did their own thing. Don't get me wrong – if I did try and talk to them they wouldn't just ignore me but they'd point out that they were busy people and I should really wait until I had something worthwhile to say. Looking back I can see where they were coming from, but at the time it left me a little bit lonely.

Being scared of going to primary school and being lonely at home is a tough combination for anyone, particularly children, but everything changed when I discovered The Lone Ranger. I remember it very well. The old Bakelite TV, the picture fuzzing at the edges and then that theme tune. Christ, it seems like yesterday. The Lone Ranger, flying about on his horse Tonto, saving all the skirt.[5] It used to break my heart when Tonto would look over at The Lone Ranger, swish his tail and call him *Kemo Sabe*.[6] I'll never forget when . . .[7]

These memories seem like yesterday inside my head but they're also tough to think about because, frankly, The Lone Ranger turned into a real monkey on my back. I get angry thinking about it even now. As far as I'm concerned it should have been made very, very clear that the show was made up and wasn't a documentary. When you're that age you pretty much take anything as gospel and that includes shows on the television. If other people, many of whom are old enough to know better, also suggest to you that a programme is based on real life then, to be fair, you're going to believe them.

The number of shoeings I picked up through The Lone Ranger years was ridiculous, but when you think The Lone Ranger has your back then you feel invincible. I'd be in the playground with all the hard nuts circling me like ants and I'd be whistling like a bastard and

5 Incorrect. The horse was called Silver, Tonto was the name given to the Lone Ranger's laconic Red Indian sidekick.
6 Tonto did use this phrase regularly but again he wasn't a horse, he was a tail-less Red Indian.
7 At this point I have deleted a further four paragraphs on Bob's memories of The Lone Ranger, all of which were inaccurate, including the protracted description of an episode where Bob misremembers The Lone Ranger making love to a string of women while Tonto (again listed as a horse) offered vocal encouragement.

looking up the Great Eastern Road and thinking 'Come on, Tonto, you're cutting this a bit fine.'

When I was ten I came home from school with the dead leg from hell and Mum finally told me that The Lone Ranger was just George Seaton in fancy dress. She said that my dead leg was a credit to George Seaton's acting and that as an amateur actor herself she hoped that one day she would be able to affect audiences in the same way.

It was very disappointing for me to hear that The Lone Ranger was a lot of bollocks and, looking back, I think this was the first example of why I haven't become the Hero of Dundee. How can you be a Hero when people get together to shaft you like that? Everyone was in on it. Mum, Dad, the kids at school, even the fucking postman who used to pretend to have a gunfight with me on his way up the path.

Let me ask you this. When your life starts with the whole world pretending that you're a cowboy and best pals with The Lone Ranger then what chance have you got?

2

Dad

My father was a great man, so everyone says. I never saw much of him but the guys that say he was a great man are all pretty decent so I've got no reason to go against their opinion. They would know better than me. I don't think it had anything to do with The Lone Ranger cock-up but Dad wasn't around much after that. He said he was working on the North Sea oil rigs, which sounds impressive enough but this was the 1950s and oil wasn't discovered in the North Sea until 1970.[8]

For a while Mum and I clung to the theory that Dad was a visionary. Unfortunately for us he was a bigamist. She should have guessed. He'd head off for two weeks with his swimming trunks, a sieve and a copy of the *Racing Post*. No-one knew much about the oil game in those days but even as a youngster I remember thinking that he must be pretty good at his job to get much oil with that gear.

Dad's other family lived in Monifieth and I always respected him for that, not having them too close to home and rubbing me and Mum's faces in it. He told us all about them eventually, which was pretty tough and must have been one of the worst anniversaries he and Mum had ever had.

It was annoying not having Dad around but, as he explained, the fifteen-minute bus journey from Monifieth was pretty boring and to be fair he always came back for his birthday. He'd arrive all excited and we'd have to get out the presents we'd got for him. It was the one thing that I remember him being strict about. The presents weren't

---

8 See *The Dundee Courier*, 10 October 1970 – '*Arrogant Aberdeen in Unlikely Oil Claim*'.

allowed to be homemade and we had to give him the receipts with them in case he wanted to take them back. I remember Mum once giving him a pink shirt and Dad said that he wasn't even going to go through what he called the pretence of taking it out the wrapping. He was always using words like that and I greatly admired him for it.

I remember the day my father died very well, largely because it was the day he died. I was sitting at my desk at school and spotted Mum in the corridor. She'd been called into the school a few weeks before after I was involved in a misunderstanding in Religious Studies and I thought that nonsense had maybe cropped up again but, no, she was there to tell me Dad had kicked the bucket.

Mum said the timing was awful because her Amateur Dramatics group were about to start a two-week run of *Oliver Twist* at the bowling club so I was to go and see Dad's other family and sort out the funeral. It was a lot of responsibility for a ten-year-old but I think Mum must have followed the Alex Ferguson policy of 'if they're good enough they're old enough'. Plus to be fair to Mum she was doing well with the Amateur Dramatics at the time despite that ridiculous stage name[9] and she'd been given the part of Fagin which is a big ask for any actor, let alone a woman.

After school I caught the bus to Monifieth and went round to see Dad's other family. His other wife wasn't home, just a lot of people I didn't know, but they told me it would be Saturday morning for the funeral. There was a depressing air about the place and I just wanted to get out but I feel bad saying that because it was a nice house and Dad had obviously put a bit of time into the garden.

The funeral was a strange old day. Mum had to go straight to a matinee so she was in her full Fagin costume which I was a bit uncomfortable with but I soon forgot about that when Dad's other wife arrived. I knew that her nickname was Bazookas and I presumed that she was maybe in the army but when she walked into the church I saw that she most definitely wasn't in the army and that wasn't why she was called Bazookas.[10]

---

9 See *The Dundee Courier*, 5 November 1954 – '*Ribeye Servant Sizzles Again*'.
10 I tracked down a photo of this woman from the period. Taken long before the era of airbrushing and other image manipulation, I was as astonished as Bob was. I discovered she died in the 1970s. When I told Bob he voiced sadness, quickly followed by speculation as to the shape of her coffin which he suggested must have looked 'like a camel'.

I'll never forget the minister's face when he came out to see the front row of me, Fagin and Bazookas. He must have thought he was part of a joke and to be fair he put on a decent show under the circumstances. After the funeral Mum and I had to rush off so she wasn't late for the matinee and I never saw Bazookas again. Sometimes I think Dad deliberately died just so I would meet her and learn a little bit about women. Usually though, I think it would probably have worked out better for me and Mum if he hadn't met Bazookas at all.

As I said, over the years a lot of people have told me Dad was a great guy but I think it's fair to say he didn't do a massive amount for Yours Truly. He did at least leave a joke in the will that was just for me. 'And give my golf clubs to my only son Brian,' he wrote.

The guy didn't even play golf.

3

Teachers Not Appreciating My Help

Getting on with teachers would have been good for me. I'd have got all my exams and gone off to shake things up as a scientist, lawyer or chat-show host. But that's not how it worked out and by the time I was twelve I'd just about had it with that lot.

As a profession (if you can call it that, they get more holidays than Alf Whicker[11]) teachers must be the most sensitive mob around. Don't get me wrong – they're not alone. When it comes to having a laugh I've never got much change out of judges and I can tell you with confidence not to waste any good slapstick on doctors. But teachers are in a different league for taking themselves seriously. They always think they know best and try and take charge of the conversation.

After The Lone Ranger problems I got sent to Bell Street Primary. With me not having much of a chance to chat at home, I saw it as an opportunity to really get things going on the conversation front, but oh no, the teachers weren't happy with that. It was an absolute joke. A lot of the stuff in school is pretty much up for debate, especially Religious Studies, but when I tried to get a wee conversation going they'd always pull the We Know Best card.

The irony is that most of the time I was trying to help the teachers and it was trying to help that would eventually get me expelled from Bell Street Primary. We had this guy Mr Conway for Maths and he was a real hopeless case. Being a teacher is about entertaining kids

---

11 I think Bob is referring to the television presenter Alan Whicker of *Whicker's World* fame.

but very few of them could hold a story and Mr Conway was the worst by far.

I saw an opportunity to both help the poor guy out and make a little something for myself so I waited behind in class and offered, very kindly, to supply some jokes to Mr Conway for 15p a time. I said that, although I obviously wouldn't name names, people were talking about him and none of it was good and this would be a chance for him to start the long journey back to respect (that was a phrase my Dad had used on me a few years before after I had an accident in my trousers and it had stuck with me ever since).

I thought that Mr Conway might haggle on the money or supply a few taboos I shouldn't cross with the jokes but in fact he reacted by clipping me on the ear. I told him, very calmly, that I had now lost any remaining respect that I had for him and he reacted by clipping me on the other ear and escorting me to the headmaster's office. I told Mr Conway that I was more disappointed in him than angry and he went a funny colour (which was the first funny thing he'd ever done) and told me to wait outside while he went in to give the headmaster his Woe Is Me act.

I wasn't too worried because I liked the headmaster and I saw a lot of myself in him. He could tell a great story for a start. Some of the assemblies were really top drawer. To this day I smile when I think of one week when he told an absolute belter about Jesus that had me off my seat at the end. I got into trouble for that, which is unbelievable really, getting into trouble for giving the Top Dog a standing ovation. That's the kind of logic I was dealing with at Bell Street Primary.

Anyway my point is that I wasn't too worried when Mr Conway stormed off and I was called in to see the headmaster. I remember really enjoying the experience because the headmaster had these leather seats in his office so sitting there talking to him felt like he was a chat-show host and I was a chat-show guest. Apart from the fact he was giving me into trouble and the fact that I was wearing shorts.

Overall, the headmaster was pretty decent. He got a bit angry when I referred to the situation as The Mr Conway Problem but I decided that was misplaced loyalty. We were getting on pretty well when he said something that nearly made me fall off my chair. He looked really tired and said that the school was full of problems and he didn't need another one. I knew exactly what he was telling me. I thanked him for his time, which he looked a bit confused about, and left.

It took me a week of hard work. I did a bit in lessons when the teachers weren't looking and then stayed up late at night which wasn't a problem because Mum was out starring in a production of *Oklahoma*.

The day I was finally ready was one I'll never forget. I got up early, did my hair really nicely, walked to school and straight into the headmaster's office. He was surprised to see me and even more surprised when I placed the folder on his desk, winked and said that A Little Birdie had told me he was looking for this. On the folder I'd written in block capitals –

BELL STREET PRIMARY – THE WAY AHEAD
By Bob Servant

I will tell you right now that for a twelve-year-old that folder was a bloody work of art. I had diagrams, sketches and some really well-written material. I'd identified the main character flaws in all the teachers, including the headmaster, and I'd also collected all the major rumours floating around, including about the headmaster. Of course, in my report I called for the firing of Mr Conway but I suggested that the headmaster saved Mr Conway embarrassment by announcing at Assembly the reason that Mr Conway wasn't at school any more was because he'd run away from home. I also had some great stuff on school lunches and was well ahead of my time by suggesting what we know today as a buffet.

I couldn't have done much more for the headmaster but, well, he didn't exactly appreciate it. Looking back, it was probably one of the best chases that I've ever been involved in but at the time it was terrifying. Luckily for me he tripped over his bin in his hurry to get round the desk at me so I had a bit of a head start. I was down the corridor and halfway through the playground by the time the headmaster made it out and shouted to a janitor to stop me.

The jannie tried to catch me but I dropped my shoulder and gave him the eyes and I was away and through the gate. Reform Street was hard work. Every time I turned round the headmaster and the jannie were closing in like ospreys. I twisted and turned my way through the shoppers and took a short cut down Bank Street past the fire station and that pet shop where the owner got done for talking dirty.[12]

I made it onto Commercial Street but by now I was getting tired and when I turned round the headmaster was only about twenty yards away. I dashed into Debenhams, ran up the stairs and found myself in the Ladieswear Department. There was a row of dresses hanging up and I slid under and got inside one. I was just in time because I could hear the headmaster arrive and ask if anyone had seen 'a little fucking lunatic' which I thought was completely inappropriate language for a headmaster to use anywhere, but especially in the Ladieswear Department.

All in all, I was inside that dress for about an hour. I have to say that, on what was otherwise a tough day for me, I enjoyed it. It was nice hearing people go about their business while I stood inside what felt like a big, flowery tent. It was my own little world where nothing bad could happen to me. Don't get me wrong − I knew I couldn't be inside the dress forever. If I'd stayed inside it forever and grown up inside the dress then at one point I would have gone from being inside the dress to wearing it and that's a different business. I waited until I couldn't hear the headmaster's voice, ducked out of the dress and made my way home feeling like someone had used my heart as a football.

Not getting the respect I deserved for

BELL STREET PRIMARY − THE WAY AHEAD
By Bob Servant

hit me hard. That folder should have made me famous and put me halfway to Hero status before I was out of shorts. I could have been a child star like Mozart, Mickey Rooney or Jimmy Krankie. But instead I was expelled and after the summer holidays I was sent to Grove Street Academy. It was the last school left for me in Broughty Ferry so I knew I had to keep my nose clean or I'd really be in trouble because Mum didn't like being bothered with what she called paperwork.

So I went to Grove Street Academy and, just when things couldn't get any worse for me, I met Frank.

---

12 See *The Dundee Courier,* 12 August 1955 − 'Pet Shop Owner Fined, Parrot Freed ("Not only have you upset a number of female customers," summed up Magistrate McLelland, "but your lies subjected a defenceless animal to a gruelling experience, one from which he or she may not recover." ').

4

Meeting Frank

Grove Street Academy was slap-bang in the middle of Broughty Ferry and very much the place to be for a thirteen-year-old. I was at the age when boys start really appreciating skirt and there was plenty of that about so when I took up my seat on the first day of term I was happy enough. Then I turned round and caught sight of Frank. Frank was funny-looking even as a kid. He wasn't one of those people who look OK as a kid then get funny-looking later, like Michael Jackson or Alf Whicker,[13] he looked funny right from the start. But it wasn't even Frank's looks that made me laugh the first time I saw him, that's how ridiculous his jumper was.

To this day Frank pretends that his school jumper had what he calls an emergency exit. The fact of the matter was that it had been knitted by his aunt who was a bad one for the gin and she'd given the thing three arms. I looked at this guy, sitting in the corner with an extra arm starting below his chin as if he was an elephant and thought, 'Jesus, we've got a live one here.'

A few days later I was walking through the playground, checking out the skirt and minding my own business, when I heard a terrible wailing. It was Frank and he wasn't wailing about his jumper but about his sandwiches. About a year before, Scotland's first-ever curry house had been opened in Dundee by a man called Bert McKintosh who had been stationed in Calcutta during the war. Dundee had only

---

13 I think Bob is again referring to the television presenter Alan Whicker but I don't really see his point. I have checked the photos in Whicker's autobiographical *Journey of a Lifetime* and don't see any great progression, negative or positive, in his looks as the years have passed.

had fish and chip shops in the past and Bengali Bertie's caused chaos because people weren't used to the spices.[14]

Looking back I think that Bengali Bertie's must have burrowed into my head like a rabbit because later I would also be a fast food revolutionary in the Cheeseburger Wars. At the time though the only effect that Bengali Bertie's had on me was through watching Frank trying to eat his sandwiches.

In those days your sandwiches at school would usually be leftovers from dinner the night before. With my mum being so busy with the Amateur Dramatics[15] I usually just kept some of my chips from dinner and stuck them in a white bap. Some of the other kids had more complicated arrangements but no-one had anything like Frank.

Frank's mum, who you'll meet shortly, was a right character. I liked her, but a lot of people thought she was a weirdo and I can see why because she used to get a wee bit obsessed with things. At the time she was obsessed with Bengali Bertie's. She'd be up there every night getting a few dishes and in the morning Frank got what was left in his sandwiches.

Right from the start Frank had told her he didn't like the food from Bengali Bertie's, so his mum used to try and trick him and he'd pull out some right crackers for lunch as a result. Corned beef nan breads, pakoras on sticks to look like toffee apples, the whole sorry business. On that particular morning his mum sprung a real belter on him, a tandoori bap which she'd said was special mince.

He'd just taken his first bite when I walked past and heard his wailing. He was in a bad state, to be fair, panting away with his tongue hanging out like a little dog. Forty years later I know that losing his dignity in public has been Frank's life work but at the time I felt sorry for the guy. I walked over, took out my Barr's Limeade and poured a very generous amount into his mouth.

'Thanks,' he said, when he'd got his breath back.

---

14 See *The Dundee Courier*, 10 July 1961 – *'Delhi Belly Kelly To Stick To Jelly* (Dundee family man Grant Kelly won't be re-visiting the controversial new Indian takeaway in Grey Street. "I won't be going there again," said Kelly yesterday, while preparing to attend his son's fifth birthday party)'.

15 See *The Dundee Courier*, 5 August 1961 – *'Where now for Extra Rare Ribeye?* ("She's outgrown us and she knows it," says Broughty Ferry Amateur Dramatics Secretary Arthur Justice.)'.

'No bother,' I said and walked off. There was quite a lot of skirt watching and I did one of those Just Doing My Job looks that are used so well on women by firemen, doctors and funeral directors. It definitely gave me a boost with the skirt, helping Frank out with the limeade, but it also made us pals.

Well, I say pals. He tried to chat to me a few times so in the end I drew up some rules. If I was talking to girls he was to stay well away because of him looking funny and if I was talking to any of the better boys then he had to do the same because of his jumper situation. Other than that, we were inseparable.

Maybe it seems unfair to say that meeting Frank was a bad thing for me and held me back. But then again maybe it doesn't because, fuck me, he's put me through the mill.

5

Mum and Uncle Harry

I remember when my Dad died I said to my Mum that it was just me and her against the world. She agreed that things weren't looking good for me but pointed out it was a bit unfair to drag her down with me. That was really her in a nutshell – she had a real can-do attitude and after Dad died she concentrated on enjoying her life. She had all that success with the Amateur Dramatics and then she concentrated on enjoying her life with Uncle Harry.

I was fifteen when Uncle Harry moved in with me and Mum. He wasn't my real uncle and I thought it was a bit much that they made me call him that, but it made them laugh and I suppose as long as someone was getting something out the joke then it wasn't all bad. It was annoying though. I was old enough to know what the two of them were up to and even if I hadn't been I would have soon worked it out because of the way Uncle Harry kept filling me in on the details.

I wouldn't have minded Uncle Harry telling me the stuff that he and Mum had been doing but the High Fives were out of order. Don't get me wrong, Uncle Harry was pretty much the first man in Dundee to regularly go for the High Five and I was glad to be part of it in that respect, but I didn't enjoy it at the time. To this day I don't really enjoy High Fives because I associate them with Uncle Harry waking me up to apologise 'for the noise' and then asking if I had 'a spare one going for the big man' and making me High Five him. This went on for about six months and things got more and more tense until Uncle Harry built the tree house.

When Uncle Harry started building me the tree house I was the happiest kid in Dundee. When he said I had to live in it I was probably the saddest. In the summer it was not too bad but once it got towards the winter it became a complete joke. I asked Mum if I could move back into the house and she said that as an artist she needed space to imagine which I suppose made sense but made me feel a bit down.

In the end I went to stay with Frank and his mum and at least they appreciated the company (Frank and his mum always told people that his dad died during the war which is a bit cheeky. The war was going on when he died but, come on, the guy had a heart attack in Debenhams).[16]

I have to say that I had a good time staying with Frank and his mum that winter. The end was in sight with school and Frank's mum had got over her Bengali Bertie's obsession and wasn't a bad cook. I suppose Frank was growing on me a little bit the way that a stray puppy would, or a winged bird, or a crippled lion. Not that Frank could ever be considered a lion, crippled or otherwise.

So I was in a decent mood when Christmas came round and Mum very kindly invited me round to the house for dinner. I hadn't seen much of her and Uncle Harry so I was excited when I stuck on my best gear, brushed my hair and headed round to the old place. We said our 'Hellos' and sat down to dinner and Mum nearly knocked me off my chair by asking if I'd ever considered emigrating to Australia.

I felt like I'd taken one in the puss from Joe Louis. Australia! I said, no, I hadn't, but I'd love to. Uncle Harry had a good laugh at that and Mum said that she'd only asked because she and Uncle Harry were emigrating to Australia and they were wondering if I had any tips.

Mum got a wee bit annoyed with me after that because she said that it was Christmas Day and the last thing she needed was to see someone crying. I apologised, and I suppose I was being a bit over the top, but by then the atmosphere was beyond repair. Mum stuck my dinner in a Tupperware box after Uncle Harry had chosen the best potatoes for himself. She suggested I eat my dinner on the way home because their cases wouldn't pack themselves.

I remember one thing she did though which always makes me smile. Uncle Harry told me to bring back the Tupperware box but Mum said that I should 'just keep it' which was a really nice touch and one that I've never forgotten. Even so, I must admit I felt a little

---

16 See *The Dundee Courier*, 18 August 1944 – '*Broughty Man's "Stubbornness" Leads to Tragedy* ("He said he'd get the trousers on if it was the last thing he did," says shop assistant Joan Downie, "but the last thing he did was to say that.")'.

bit sad on the walk home to Frank's that night. He and his mum gave me a decent welcome but my heart wasn't in it so I went up to bed.

The arrangement was that I slept in Frank's bed and he slept on the floor beside me because, as I told him, I was the guest. That night, the last night I saw my Mum, Frank waited till I was nearly asleep and then whispered, 'Don't worry, Bob, you'll always have me.'

I don't think I've ever felt as low in my whole life as when Frank said that. He really put the boot in.

6

Joining the Merchant Navy

Joining the Merchant Navy wasn't one of those good ideas you have that turn out not to be a good idea, like a picnic or a side parting. It was one of those good ideas that wasn't even a good idea in the first place. Needless to say, it was Frank's idea.

It was the spring of 1962. I was sixteen, already wowing the skirt, and had eyes like Omar Sharif. I could have done anything. Finished school, entered a trade, or trained to be a chat-show host. But no, for the first and last time I listened to Frank.

I got up to go to school one day and Frank was nearly hyperventilating. I was worried because he was ironing my uniform at the time. His hands were all shaky so I said he could have a short break and tell me what had wound him up. He said he'd just heard on the wireless that the Merchant Navy had set up a training centre in Dundee and suggested me and him should join up.

I told Frank to count to twenty then get back to the ironing while I had my bath. I have to say I was interested. I'd read a bit about the Navy in comics and it certainly offered more excitement than taking on an apprenticeship or going into the Dog Eat Dog hell of the mousetrap factory. At breakfast I said it was a possibility. Frank was buttering my toast at the time and nearly took off a finger but his Mum said she wasn't sure. She said I shouldn't leave school this close to my exams because I was clever enough to pass them and she said Frank shouldn't leave school because he needed the supervision.

I pointed out that I was unlikely to pass my exams because I was dedicating most of my time to chasing skirt and that Frank would get a lot better supervision in the Merchant Navy than anywhere else. Frank's mum wasn't the brightest – it was only a few months since Frank and I did that torch trick on her[17] – and the two of us soon talked her round.

We went into school and told them we were quitting that same day. The teacher said I was wasting my life and I said that one day I would be back to show him my medals and walked out with my head held high and all the skirt looked at me with big eyes. Frank shouted that one day he'd be back to show the teacher his gun which provoked a different reaction and I heard some screaming and then Frank ran past me and I met him back at the house.

The next day Frank and I caught the bus up to the docks and there's no doubt we were both a little nervous. When we actually got to the training centre, though, we were absolutely delighted. It was a big warehouse with all these bits of ships, and ropes and big maps on tables. Best of all was that in the corner there was a row of uniforms. 'Look, Bob,' said Frank, 'uniforms.'

It was a wonderful moment. These days it seems just about anyone gets a decent uniform. I saw a traffic warden recently who looked like he'd just got back from Iraq. But back then it was hard to get hold of a uniform and when you did get one, no matter how shite is was, the skirt thought you were in the SAS. And now here were Frank and myself on the verge of getting hold of some of the best uniforms going. Just when we thought it couldn't get any better we met Alf Whicker.[18]

---

17 See *The Dundee Courier* 16 January 1962 – '*Broughty Woman "Embarrassed" Over UFO "Mix-Up".*'
18 Oh, right, hang on.

7

Alf Whicker

Alf Whicker was an interesting guy. As a kid he'd apparently been a right looker and took the Bonniest Baby cup in the Broughty Ferry Gala Week. Then he'd run away at fifteen to join the Merchant Navy and this was him back in Dundee to set up a training centre. He'd certainly seen a bit of life. His face was all red from the sea and he had scars and tattoos and, if truth be told, Frank and I were both impressed by the guy. And that was before he started talking skirt.[19]

Alf got all the boys together and reeled off these stories about going round the world and some of the sights he'd seen. He talked about how he'd been to islands where the local women wore grass skirts and Frank and I nearly keeled over when he described them. I mean, if you'd made grass skirts for some of the women that Frank I are were chasing in those days you'd be talking about rolling up bowling greens but the way Alf Whicker put it we were going to have a cracker of a wife in every port. 'Hopefully not in Tayport!' I joked and Alf Whicker told me in no uncertain terms that I wasn't allowed to make jokes.

He was a tough guy, was Alf Whicker. He talked so much about foreign places that Frank and I used to say that he wasn't really Alf Whicker, he was Tony Whicker[20] off the television but we always kept our voices down.

Things started not too bad for me and Frank at the Merchant

---

19 OK, disregard all previous references to the television presenter Alan Whicker. Bob was indeed referring to an Alf Whicker.
20 I think Bob is referring to the television presenter Alan Whicker.

Navy. The first few weeks was rope stuff, learning the bits of boats and reading maps. It was when we had what's called the On Land Exam after three months that everything went wobbly. Guess whose fault that was?

Frank had promised me he'd been paying attention. After every day I'd say, 'So you got that?' and he'd tap the side of his head and say 'Locked down, Bob, locked down.' Soon I'd learn that if Frank taps his head and says anything at all it should be cause for alarm but back then I was still learning and probably enjoying the course too much to notice Frank was toiling.

Unfortunately for me, the two of us had been paired up and you had to sit the exams together. The night before the exam I suggested we go over a few things and Frank got a bit nervous. Then I started testing him and he folded like a pack of cards. He was crying and kind of hitting himself quite hard in the legs and calling himself stupid and saying he was hopeless and all this.

I have to say I didn't handle it brilliantly. For the first hour or two I was largely agreeing with him and suggesting other things he should call himself and other places he should hit himself. Then I realised that he was going to take me down with him and I suppose seeing any man like that does something to you, so I told Frank to pull himself together and we started revising. We were up most of the night and even on the bus to the training centre I was showing him knots.

Alf Whicker got everyone together and explained the process. The On Land Exam was one day and if you passed you got to do the Open Water Exam the next day at the Monikie Reservoir. If you passed that you were in, you got your uniform and you were off to the High Seas. 'And you know what happens there, don't you, lads?" said Alf Whicker and gave one of those winks that weather forecasters do when they want you to know they're really talking about sex.

First up was the maps and I managed to sneak Frank a look at my sheet so we got through that OK. Then was the parts of boats which I had written right up Frank's arm and he managed to not make it too obvious he was looking. Then came the knots and Alf Whicker announced we all had to do a reverse rolling hitch double bend which, as some of you might know, is the Hitler of the knot world. It's an absolute bugger of a thing to do and it took me a good while to get mine together. By the time I turned round to help Frank it was all too late.

To this day I don't know how he managed to do what he'd done. The rope was in these big wild loops on the floor and then all over Frank. He'd got one of his feet tied up near his arse, his other leg had the rope wrapped round his knee and then his upper body was twisted to the side because the rope was round his neck. He was sweating badly, possibly because of the pressure of the exam or possibly because of the rope round his neck and was kind of whispering, 'Help me, Bob, Jesus, Bob, help me,' over and over again.

Before I could sort it out Alf Whicker shouted 'You!' and marched over to Frank. I was already starting to pack up my things and Frank, surprise surprise, had already started to cry when Alf Whicker asked 'When did you go to Tahiti?'

It turned out that Frank had tied an arrangement that was an exact replica of something used by dolphin fishermen in Tahiti. Whicker told us they tied themselves like that so they're not thrown off their canoes when they hook a dolphin and that it had taken him two months to learn how to tie the knot himself. Frank was gibbering away, and his leg was clearly losing circulation, so I cleverly stepped in and said that Frank and I had learnt it together from a fisherman in Arbroath.

Alf looked at us both, said he'd never been prouder, and that he'd see us tomorrow at Monikie Reservoir. What a moment. Frank and I were singing on the bus home that night and the next day we rolled up at Monikie, one day away from joining the Merchant Navy.

8

Not Joining the Merchant Navy

One day, that's all we had to do. One day and we'd be in the Merchant
Navy. Christ, even now I get hot and bothered thinking about that
day at Monikie. I go up there sometimes, for a nice walk with skirt
or to have a wee fish with a pal and every time I'll say, 'Did I ever tell
you when Frank fucked up the Merchant Navy for me here?' Usually
my pal will say, 'Yeah, you have.' Sometime the pal's Frank and if
it is then I make him listen to it all over again.

We got there early and each pair was given a rowing boat and a
map. There were all these buoys in the reservoir and you had to go
between them in a certain route while Alf Whicker watched from
the shore. We set off and it seemed we were doing OK. Frank did the
navigating and I pulled away at the oars with my muscles and I have
to say I was quietly confident at that point because none of the other
boats seemed to be anywhere near us. Then we went round a buoy
and Frank turned really quiet. He took out the emergency paddle and
tied it to the side of the boat pointing outwards. I asked what he was
doing and he stood up and passed me the map.

'I've been holding it upside down, Bob,' he told me, and I saw that
he had. I was angry but more confused and I asked again what he
was doing. 'I've let you down for the last time, Bob,' he said. 'I'm
walking the plank.'

Sometimes Frank does something so stupid that I genuinely don't
know what to say and that was probably the first such occasion. Before
I had a chance to stop him he said, 'Let them eat cake,' stepped onto
the paddle and upended the entire boat. The cold of the water was
a bit of a shock but the truth of the matter is that we weren't exactly
in much danger. I think that's what has always annoyed me the most

about Frank walking the plank, the fact that we were about five yards from shore at the time. Back when it was popular, walking the plank was one of the most dangerous things you could do at sea but you're not exactly going to get picked off by sharks five yards from shore. Not at Monikie.

Anyway, Alf Whicker pulled us out, called us a disgrace and sent us packing. I've had some depressing bus journeys in my life but that one has to be right up there, seeing as I was dripping wet, kicked out the Merchant Navy and sitting next to Frank. I didn't speak to him the whole way home and sent him to Coventry for a week which of course he misunderstood and his mum only just got to the train station in time.

I still call him Frank The Plank to remind him but to be honest I think that's lenient because what a start the Merchant Navy could have given me, both in my life and in becoming a Hero. It was my chance to see the world and Frank stole it from me. Don't get me wrong – I went to Newcastle for Tommy Peanut's Divorce Party, and there was a lot of talk in the nineties about Spain but it came to nothing after Frank lost his passport in a door-to-door confidence scam.

But that's not really seeing the world and even if I'd just gone round the world then came back to Dundee I'd have had a great reception. When Chappy Williams went to Canada to see his uncle people talked about him like he was Christopher Columbus and the guy only went because he got the tickets free with his Hoover. But that's what it's like in Dundee – people admire anyone from the city who goes on and grabs international glory because so few of us have cracked it. Off the top of my head I can only think of Brian Cox, Gorgeous George Galloway and that guy from Monifieth who throttled a waiter in Magaluf.[21] That's a gang that I should have been part of and I would have been if it wasn't for Frank The Plank.

The world would have been my oyster. More to the point, I might have made some black pals.

---

21 See *The Dundee Courier*, 4 May 1987 – '*Shifty Spaniard Tricks Monifieth Man Into So-called Strangling*'.

9

Not Having Any Black Pals

I'm going to put this one in here before I forget. I don't have any black pals whatsoever, and, let me tell you this, it's not through lack of trying. For longer than I care to remember I have tried like a bastard to get myself a friend who's a bit more exotic than the average and all I've ended up doing is running into brick walls. I won't hear a word said against Dundee as a city but there's no doubt that we don't have the exciting mix of other places. To be fair, things are getting a bit more interesting now but for years if a black guy popped up in Dundee it was like Beatlemania and we'd be all over him like a cheap suit.

In 1972 we were out doing the windows when Frank got hit on the head by a bucket. There was just the two of us there, and I was directly above him at the time but to this day I won't take any responsibility for insurance reasons. As I've told him over the years when these things crop up, there is his truth, my truth and the insurance form.

However it happened, Frank caught a bucket square on the napper and went down like he'd been shot. Considering how often he fell off the ladder it wasn't exactly a cause for concern so I patched him up using my spare vest but he whined away like he always does and I had to drive him up to Ninewells Hospital. We're talking about the seventies, when the NHS got itself into hot water and brought over a few boys from Africa to help with the waiting lists.[22] Frank was away with the fairies from the bang on his head so I was having a bit

---

22 See *The Dundee Courier*, 15 May 1972 – '*Do We Ken-ya Face?*' and 26 May 1972 – '*A Mala-wee Surprise for Local Woman*, ("I went in for my veins but felt like I was on an exciting safari holiday" said Dorothy Chambers, 57.)'.

of fun with him, telling him it was Christmas Day and he'd won the Spot The Ball and so on, when this African doctor popped up.

Frank and I were gobsmacked and I have to say I was a little tongue-tied. I managed to get that he was from Kenya but after that it was really just business. I did get one joke in. When he was bandaging up Frank's face I told him to wrap the whole lot up because I was sick of looking at it. It was only a wee joke, just something to get the ball rolling really, but he didn't have the chance to come back with a joke of his own because Frank started playing up. He was an absolute disgrace – giggling away at everything the doctor said and then making sure to give his phone number to the doctor who said about five times that he didn't need it.

For the next week or two Frank was unbearable. Every time his phone went he said, 'Oh, that might be my Kenyan pal,' and then he announced that he didn't want to watch *Zulu* on Sunday afternoons anymore because he had 'split loyalties'. He was completely smitten and I suppose I should hold my hands up to a degree and say that he wasn't alone.

I had started secretly hanging about Ninewells looking for the doctor. When I write that now I'm fairly embarrassed but it was a decision that I made at the time and I just have to deal with it. The guy had got into my head and sometimes that's the way it is with new pals.

It took a few trips but eventually I spotted him leaving one evening. I followed him to the bus stop where he caught the 18 to Lochee. That's the wrong side of town for me but I wasn't thinking straight. The next night I got on the 18 one stop up so when he arrived I was ready for him with the old 'Oh, it's yourself, I was just thinking about you there' routine. He was a bit surprised and I sort of had to remind him who I was but after that it wasn't too bad.

It became a daily thing and after a week or two we were running out of conversation. Well, I was anyway, he didn't really have much to start with. He was never up for a quick drink. I asked every night and started getting off at his stop to put on the pressure. He wouldn't even entertain the idea, even the day I said I'd lost my keys and it would maybe make sense for me to stay at his house. Fair enough, some guys don't like going for a drink but I still think it's totally out of order to just walk away when a man tells you something like that. Particularly when he's crying.

Luckily that night really shook me back to my senses and I left him alone afterwards. There's been bits and pieces with other guys over the years but nothing concrete. I put up a sign at Safeways looking for a black pal but they took it down because of discrimination, which didn't add up. There was a Turkish guy who worked at The Fort bar who I had a bit of a chat with on occasion but only ever as part of a larger group and it was never just me and him. Chappy's uncle came over from Canada for the Millennium and I got on well with him. He wasn't black though.

My point here, and it's an important one, is that I always think that I'd have traditionally been seen as more of a man of the world if I'd had black pals. I could have got some early doors through the Merchant Navy and that doctor would have been absolutely perfect but it didn't work out in either case and there's no doubt that's cost me. I mean, you look at the guys I've hung about with over the years and they're not exactly the Harlem Globetrotters.

10

Finding Stewpot's

I found Stewpot's bar in the summer of 1963. Sometimes Frank says he found it, which is laughable. We were seventeen at the time and a few months off being legal so you had to pick and choose your boozers quite carefully. I would have been OK on my own – I was six feet tall and walked like Errol Flynn – but Frank looked like he should still be in shorts and the tragedy is that he often was.

It's not that we didn't have money for better clothes. Between us we were doing four paper rounds, which sounds impossible but not with the system that I put in. Frank went and did the paper rounds and I waited for him to come home and then collected the money, did the accounts and advised him on any problems he might have encountered that morning.

Sometimes Frank would complain about doing all the legwork and I'd be very patient and explain again the meaning of the phrase 'horses for courses'. If he kept going with the Woe Is Me stuff then I'd point out that he did more paper rounds than anyone in Dundee, he was the paper-round champion, and if turning someone into a champion was a bad thing then someone should tell the boy that trains Cassius Clay to close the gym.

On a Friday night we'd usually head to the Cuckoo's Nest pub on the Claypotts Roundabout. It wasn't exactly Las Vegas down there – it was bloody dangerous to get to for a start[23] – but we could always

---

23 See *The Dundee Courier,* 17 January 1963 – '*Pub Marooned On City's First Roundabout* (Dundee City Council's Planning Committee today denied that there had been "serious gaps" in their knowledge of the country's new roundabout system.)'.

get served because the Cuckoo's Nest barman Terry Devine had
fallen out with a chip pan and could only just see out of one eye. Me
and Frank put on deep voices, which was a lot harder for him than
me, and we got served every time. Getting your drink could take a
while if the place was busy but it was a good atmosphere with Terry
feeling his way along the optics and everyone giving it the 'warmer,
colder' routine.

But Frank and I wanted somewhere a bit more happening and,
to be honest with you, with a better level of skirt. For the first few
years after it opened the Claypotts roundabout was unbelievably
busy because of the novelty factor[24] and it was impossible for any
skirt wearing heels to beat the traffic. The women that made it to the
Cuckoo's Nest were largely women who were addicted to danger and
although women like that are good to talk to (or listen to in the case
of Tina Turner) they're not usually relationship material.

We'd heard of Stewpot's, of course, it was a big name back then
on the pub scene just like it is today. I knew my dad used to drink
there and that the owner had named if after his son, so one Friday
night we were leaving the house for the Cuckoo's Nest when I said,
'Forget the Cuckoo's Nest, Frank, we're going to Stewpot's.' His face
went like tomato ketchup and he said we'd never get in but using my
eyes I told him not to worry.

We went past Safeways, through the Long Lane and up past Toshy's
Hardware. You could hear the laughter from fifty yards away. We
walked in and there we were – me and Frank standing in Stewpot's
for the very first time. I'll never forget the landlord's words. He said,
'Have you two lost your football or something?' and that was the first
time that men laughed with me in Stewpot's bar.

Unfortunately Frank missed the fact that we were involved in a
joke with the landlord and started saying that he had lost his ball
in Dawson Park and if it had shown up in Stewpot's then he was
willing to take it back without any questions being asked and on
and on even though I was giving him a look that said 'stop talking
immediately'.

---

24 See *The Dundee Courier*, 26 March 1963 – '*Inverness Couple Delighted With
Roundabout Trip* (". . . everything we hoped for and more . . . it's like being on the
moon.")'.

The landlord was about to chuck us out, and I couldn't blame him, when I said how I thought my dad used to drink there and said his name and the landlord and the others all looked happy and said what a good guy he was and was I the kid with the pony? I said that maybe that was someone from Dad's other family and they all kind of looked at their drinks and the landlord went nervous and said we could come in any time and why didn't we meet his son? Then he shouted 'Stewpot' and over came this lad with a nice face.

Stewpot was the same age as us but even then he carried himself very differently. Like any great diplomat – your Ghandis, Mandelas, your Lynams – Stewpot has a manner about him that relaxes people and takes the sting out of the situation. I've always said that if anyone from the Ferry took hostages and held off police in an armed siege then I would want Stewpot sent in as the lead negotiator.

(Unfortunately I've never had the chance for that theory to be tested but I have high hopes for a guy who works at Safeways. He's in the Territorial Army and he's always angry. I've heard him swearing at the vegetable section, really laying into them on a personal level, and once caught him beating up a trolley in the car park. 'Must make you feel like taking a few hostages?' I said hopefully to him that day in the car park but he pretended not to know what I was saying. It would be nice to know if taking hostages at least featured in the guy's plans but it's a hard thing to bring up. I suppose taking hostages is something that people do at very short notice for security reasons so I'll just have to wait and see if it pans out or not. But if the guy from Safeways does take hostages, and as I said it's not guaranteed, I have absolutely no doubt that it should be Stewpot sent in to negotiate, with me offering support and Frank locked in his house.)

Having said all that, just because he's my tip as a hostage negotiator doesn't mean I think that Stewpot's perfect – far from it. He didn't exactly get much of a handle on my Gin Crisis, which we'll come to, and I suppose if we're going to nitpick then we'd point out Stewpot sold me a fair portion of the gin but that's business and when I had the cheeseburger vans I sold Slim Smith more burgers than I care to remember and that was after he'd given up stairs. Not only is Stewpot a businessman, though, he's also a bloody good one. He's got the timeshare in Pitlochry, the Sierra and more nice jumpers than anyone I know. He doesn't flaunt his money which, being a self-made man myself (with a lot of money), I very much respect.

The only time I've ever seen Stewpot flustered was when Frank's nephew showed him that thing on the Internet[25] and Stewpot went shaky, called them 'faceless cowards', stormed down to the cellar and, rumour has it, kicked the living daylights out of a sack of lemons.

All in all, Stewpot is one of life's diamonds and I've had forty-seven years of good times in his pub (his dad gave him Stewpot's for his 21st birthday and went off to run a bed and breakfast in Carnoustie that I would infamously attack with an airgun during The Gin Crisis) but even then I must admit there's days when I wonder if Stewpot's bar is one of the reasons I've not made the big time. Going there pretty much every day all these years must have cost me a bit of time if you add it up and there's no-one who goes to Stewpot's every day that's really made it at an international level.

On the other side of the coin I've got great memories of the place and I suppose I've made some alright pals from going there. But on the other side of the coin[26] I could argue that those forty-seven years have boiled down to forty-seven years' worth of stupid jokes from Chappy Williams, Tommy Peanuts moaning about Sally Peanuts and Frank asking Stewpot if there's 'any surprises on the sandwich menu'.

Still, back in 1963 we were pleased enough to find it and we celebrated Frank's 18th birthday there shortly after. Not that he remembered.

---

25 See TripAdvisor.com's sparse Dundee section for an April 2004 review written by *Dusseldorf1976* entitled *The Worst Day Of Our Lives Yet!* ('We thought that this place was a traditional Scottish cafeteria but this was not the case. The people were not like people that we expect to ever meet again. The men were angry and had faces red not from the sun and shouted even when they stood close. There were not any women we do not think.')

26 I hope Bob has kept this physics-defying coin in a safe place.

Frank's 18th Birthday[27]

11

Chappy Williams and Tommy Peanuts

I remember the first time I met Chappy Williams very well. He walked into Stewpot's wearing a golf jumper and looking like he owned the place and me and Frank sat there and thought, 'Look at this prick.' And you know what? Nearly fifty years later, if you were to come down Stewpot's bar, you'd find Chappy walking in there wearing a golf jumper and looking like he owns the place and me and Frank sitting there thinking, 'Look at this prick.'

Chappy was fairly well known at the time because he was a champion schoolboy golfer so he was always in the paper holding up trophies and doing the old Look At Me routine. We spoke to him a bit that night and to be fair he wasn't too bad with the talking and the jokes and from then on we'd always have a bit of a To And Fro when he came in. That's not to say he wasn't a pain in the arse from the start. He'd practise his swing at the urinals which was both annoying and dangerous and when you shook his hand he'd say things like 'Don't steal my grip' or 'You're crushing the moneymaker'.

Because of that nonsense I wasn't too bothered when Chappy's golfing career came to a sudden halt, though I have to say I did feel sorry for him on a man-to-man level. He got to the final of the Scottish Amateur Open and whoever wins that usually flies into the professional game. But around the world there can't be more than a handful of golfers who have seen their whole career crumble in front of their eyes because of Tony Jacklin farting and Chappy was just unlucky to be one of them.[28]

---

28 See *The Dundee Courier*, 8 September 1966 – '*Chaos Reigns At The Scottish Amateur Open* (The Scottish Amateur Open was thrown into disarray yesterday when the nation's two leading youth hopes, Dundee's Chappy Williams and

After the Jacklin incident Chappy became the professional at Broughty Ferry Golf Club and he was there for forty years until his retirement.[29] Well, there and in Stewpot's by three o'clock every afternoon. We've had a few ups and down over the years but all in all I suppose Chappy's a pal.

Unlike Chappy Williams, Tommy Peanuts has never really been any trouble at all. He was already with Sally when he started coming into Stewpot's and the two of them were an OK couple. He didn't try and act like he was Burt Lancaster just because he'd got a girlfriend like some guys do and back then he'd just started at the insurance company and he was OK about talking about that as well.

It was in the early 1980s that myself, Frank and Chappy had to have a bit of a chat with Tommy after he'd got a few promotions and made the mistake that people who work in offices sometimes make when they think that you would like to hear what they do when they're in the offices. You'd ask him how he was getting on and he'd start telling us about things that had happened in his office, and meetings he'd had when he'd had to 'shake things up' or that he was 'having a problem with the Johnston account' and me, Frank and Chappy looked at each other and thought, 'Is he having a fucking laugh?' In the end we sat him down and said we were happy he'd got his promotions and so on but he should only really talk about stuff that happened in his office to other people in his office. And, to be fair to Tommy, he held his hands up and agreed. That's the only problem we've ever had with Tommy but back in the sixties he was great and he and Sally were good fun. For Frank, Chappy and myself, seeing those two together probably helped kick off The Great Skirt Hunt.

Edinburgh's Tony Jacklin were locked in a bitter feud. As officials tried to regain control Williams could be heard accusing Jacklin of an unorthodox distraction tactic as Williams attempted a vital putt. "He knew exactly what he was doing," said Williams (20) last night. "It was a low, controlled noise. Like a trumpet. I hope he's happy with himself." Jacklin said the accusation was "ludicrous" and added, "Things happen on a golf course, just like things happen in life.")'.

29 See *The Dundee Courier*, 3 December 2006 – '*Retiring Broughty Golfing Legend Offers Olive Branch To Jacklin* ("I'd like to thank all the members for forty wonderful years . . . It still hurts, there's no doubt about that and it's probably gone on too long. Pick up the phone, Tony.").

12

The Great Skirt Hunt

The Great Skirt Hunt started in 1965 and lasted a couple of years. Frank and I were doing bits and pieces with work, I was on the milk for a while for Big Sandy and then the two of us did six months out on the berries which was a good job because the sun made me look like Rock Hudson (and Frank look like a bell-end) and we had weekends off to hit the town.

By 1965 we were getting good at hitting the town and talking to skirt and we looked not too bad at all with the corduroy and so on but we decided we needed a final touch. Women have always liked a man with a gimmick – just look at Rod Hull or Mussolini – and for me and Frank I suggested we head up to Simpson's Silver in Monifieth.

These days Simpson has that big place in the town and he's in the paper all the time with his advert.[30] Whenever the advert's in the paper I show the boys in Stewpot's and say 'More like Bin Laden's cave.'

Chappy always waits till the laughter's stopped and then claims he made that joke about Simpson's advert back in the nineties. As I point out to him, Bin Laden's only hit the big time since 9/11 but according to Chappy he 'heard whispers' about Bin Laden before then. But even if he had, and he hadn't, then there's no way that any of us would have understood the joke and I would have remembered the fall-out for sure because it would have led to a day full of questions, debate and a few people going home in the huff. Just like 9/11.

(That's an example of a joke when you say something for Shock Value. I'm very good at it but if you're thinking of trying it then pick

---

30 See multiple copies of *The Dundee Courier* – *'Come to My Aladdin's Cave!'*

your audience carefully. Put it this way, I tried it once at a funeral and the response was absolutely pathetic.) [31]

Anyway, to kick off The Great Skirt Hunt, Frank and I headed up to Simpson's Silver which back then was just Simpson selling jewellery out his garage. He showed us these two silver chains which, to be fair, looked the bee's knees and he told us they were just off the boat from London. I suppose it should have appeared suspicious that anything would come from London by boat but we fell for Simpson's patter and took them off his hands.

What a joke those chains were. Frank's neck had turned green by the time we'd got back to the Ferry and I wore mine in the bath and it started fizzing and giving off heat. As I said to Frank, after we put the chains in the bin, if Simpson had just told me that the chain would fizz and give off heat when it encountered water then I could have built that into a story or a magic trick, but for it to happen when it was just me and the chain in the bath was a completely wasted opportunity.

We didn't need the chains anyway. It sounds daft but even Frank was getting some attention at the time and that always cheered me up because things went so badly for him. Probably the thing that held him back the most was his habit with skirt that if he didn't think they were listening to his stories he would tap them on the top of the head, which didn't exactly work in his favour. He also put far too much pressure on himself and if things started to go wrong he'd completely overreact, like the time he took some skirt to Dawson Park on a picnic but forgot the plates and it took her three hours to talk him down from the climbing frame.

To be fair to Frank, if I must, I was having my own problems.

---

31 See *The Dundee Courier*, 28 August 1987 – '*Local Man's Zombie Act Disrupts Funeral,* ("For me, I played the right joke to the wrong crowd," said Servant, 41)'.

13

Women Not Saying What They Mean

Over the years I've got used to the fact that women can be a bit funny about saying what they really mean. It used to annoy me but these days it just makes me laugh and if anything I feel sorry for them. Women say bad things to me and I just nod and smile and say, 'Oh really? I'm an idiot am I?' and I shake my head and do that thing with my eyes that veteran police detectives do when they're in the interview room and having to listen to the same old defence from the murderer that they've heard a thousand times before. Back at the time of The Great Skirt Hunt, however, I was still very much finding my feet and learning tough lessons by the day.

The incident that caused me big problems started off innocent enough. I was at The Sands Disco down at the Esplanade with Frank and Chappy. Chappy was off talking to some boys from the golf club and I couldn't see Frank so I thought I'd go and do what I could on the dance floor. I was just about holding my own when this decent bit of skirt with the most wonderful golden hair started giving me the old smile and look away and then quickly look back stuff. So I started giving her the old smile then frown and then the roll of the eyes and the wink. Then she started a tactic I hadn't seen before where she looked a bit to my side and looked scared. I turned to my side and, fuck my luck, it was Frank.

Frank dancing is violent stuff, all kicks and karate chops and lots of eye contact, and it tends to alarm people who haven't seen it before. That night in The Sands my new skirt looked petrified but I was sharp as a tack and went over and shouted to her, 'I'll have one of what he's having,' and pointed at Frank. Saying, 'I'll have one of what he's having,' and pointing at someone is one of those jokes that's useful in loads of situations. I'd say that in my time I've used it on over a thousand occasions. Off the top of my head the best times I've used it were – when David Icke was on Wogan, when Saddam Hussein invaded Kuwait and when that guy got electrocuted by the cigarette machine in Stewpot's though I should say I didn't realise he was being electrocuted when I made the joke.

As always the reception to the 'I'll have one of what he's having' joke was positive and me and my new skirt made our way to the bar. I bought her a drink and went to work with the jokes and the stories. It was hard because of the music so I did some physical stuff including the Buster Keaton one of pretending to walk down a flight of stairs that don't exist although in all honesty that one didn't work particularly well so I pretended I'd dropped my change from the drinks.

She let me see her up the road and I couldn't take my eyes off her golden hair which looked really top class in the moonlight and she lived in the new flats on Forthill Road, which impressed me because by all accounts they were pretty space-age. I got a wee kiss and did a bit of patting and so on and she said that she hoped she'd see me again. Hold tight, I thought, and I suggested we did something the next day. She said she had to go to work (I can't remember what, but it's not vital to the narrative) [32] but we could do something together in the evening. I asked what and she said, 'Surprise me,' and did that sort of saucy, Anything's Possible look that you used to get a lot in the *Carry On* films and from other passengers in the early days of inter-city trains.

I knew exactly what to do. The next day I went up to her flat when she was at work and got in through a window. I took off all my clothes and waited for her in her bed, lying there like a Roman Emperor and with cheekbones like Bobby Moore. After a while lying there like a Roman Emperor with my balls out started to get a bit boring so I had

---

32 This is a phrase Bob enjoys using after I taught him it during the first book we wrote together (he had included a 500-word description of his eyes and the various messages they are capable of sending to others). For many months after Bob would gain his revenge on the cutting of his eye capabilities by interrupting anything I was saying with a raised hand and 'is it vital to the narrative?' accompanied by his wink. Bob's winking style, I should quickly add, is of some interest. Not only does he wink, he points at his eye while doing so in case anyone in attendance has missed the comic gesture.

a wee wander round her space-age flat. She had a bottle of OVD and the way I saw it she'd offer me a drink when she got back anyway so I might as well get the party started sort of thing.

After that there's a bit of a gap. I remember dancing in her space-age living room and bits and pieces but the next thing you know I was lying asleep on her bed and then there was a key in the door and I woke up and I was lying on the bed wearing one of her dresses and a wonderful golden wig. To this day I maintain two things. I was obviously cold and too drunk to find my clothes and that's her fault for having a space-age flat with no central heating. And I'd obviously found the wig and been so annoyed about being duped about her wonderful golden hair that I'd put it on to teach her a lesson and that's pretty much fair enough.

She came into her bedroom and she had short, ginger hair like a fairground worker and I was just about to give her into trouble for lying about her hair situation when she saw me and, well. I did my best, I pointed at the dress and did a face as to say, 'It's just a joke, don't even worry about it,' but she ignored my face's message and let rip.

Sweet Jesus, the noise that woman made. Well, I don't even know if you could call it a scream. Years later Frank I were watching a documentary about monkeys and one of them turned on the cameraman and let out this noise and I near enough had a heart attack because it was exactly the noise the woman made at the Forthill Flats. It went on and on and on. A few weeks later an old milkman colleague of mine told me that they'd heard her from Big Sandy's Barnhill Dairy, which is about half a mile away.

I tried to calm her down with a bit of 'calm down' stuff with my hands but it didn't have any effect and to be honest I lost patience with her. It was a complete over-reaction to what was glorified slapstick and who knows the damage it was doing to my eardrums so in the end I just walked out. I was so angry with the woman for her nonsense that I was halfway down Forthill Road before I thought it would have been a good idea to have changed back into my own clothes but by then I'd passed the point of no return so I took my heels – sorry, her heels – off and started running.

I got past Safeways without seeing anyone, which was my big fear, but then I turned into me and Frank's road and I saw him come out the house towards me. I crossed the road and put my head down and ran full pace past him, got round the corner and peeked back. He was standing watching where I'd been for a while then he wandered off. I slipped back along the pavement, into the house and straight upstairs to get washed, changed and chuck the woman's clothes in the bin.

Frank was in a great mood over dinner, laughing away at my jokes even more than usual and telling his mum how nice the potatoes were. He asked if me and him could go for a drink afterwards and I agreed reluctantly because it was looking from his excitement that he'd come up with a new system to beat Spot The Ball.

I wish it had been Spot The Ball. We sat down with our drinks in the Cuckoo's Nest's beer garden and above the noise of the traffic Frank shouted that he'd met someone or maybe not met someone but seen someone he liked. A bus went round the roundabout so I missed some of it but then he was saying how this woman was top drawer and he'd seen her in the street and she had a 'lovely running style' and 'wonderful golden hair'.

I felt sick to my stomach and the worst thing was I couldn't even give Frank into trouble for making me sick to my stomach because then I'd have had to tell him the whole shebang. So I just had to deal with it, which was tough because he spent weeks looking for what he called his 'Barefoot Bombshell' and I had to pretend to keep an eye out for her myself.

When you're spending your time looking out for a woman that your pal fancies when that woman was actually you dressed as a woman then it's hard to move on with your life and be a Hero. I suppose you're some sort of Hero to your pal but only if you're willing to spend time with him dressed as a woman. Each to their own and all that, but that has to be just about the last kind of Hero that I'd want to be.

14

Lord Dundee's Lover

I remember once reading that Shakin' Stevens' biggest regret was not taking on the American market in a determined way, rather than just playing the odd showcase gig and appearing on couple of cable chat shows, and I often think about *Lord Dundee's Lover* in much the same way. For me *Lord Dundee's Lover* was an opportunity as big as the moon and twice as important but I gave up after one setback and for that I only have myself and Frank to blame.

You probably won't have heard of *Lord Dundee's Lover* so let me ask you this instead – have you heard of *Lady Chatterley's Lover,* the famous saucy novel? Aye, you have, of course you have. And then some. Well, let me tell you a little secret. If I'd only held my nerve against the boo boys in Stewpot's then *Lord Dundee's Lover* would have been just as famous as *Lady Chatterley's Lover* and about three times as successful.

It all came about because of the stuff in the papers back then concerning *Lady Chatterley's Lover.* The Government were acting like Jesus and saying how people would lose their minds if they read the book and there were all these protests until they stopped being fannies and let it be sold in the shops. None of the shops in Dundee would touch it, the manager of Woolworth's came out on his high horse and said how Dundee folk wouldn't stand for it and every single person in Stewpot's pointed out that not only would they very much stand for it, so would the manager of Woolworth's who we'd all seen give Dorothy Slaughterhouse the old octopus hands treatment at The Sands when his wife was in Ninewells with angina.

Anyway, from bitter experience,[33] I happened to know that if you

---

33 During the edit, Bob clarified that he had ordered *The Big Book of British Birds* from the Broughty Ferry library at the age of fifteen, only to be disappointed that the book arrived with no photos of females 'British or otherwise'.

went to Broughty Ferry library and ordered any book from the list they had to get in one copy. Frank and I went up there and ordered *Lady Chatterley's Lover* and oh dear the atmosphere was appalling but they had to do it. A week later we went and spent another tough morning picking it up. Watching the old bird behind the counter get *Lady Chatterley's Lover* from the shelf to the desk using a pair of spoons was one of the most painful hours of my life but when I offered to help she said I'd done enough damage already and gave me a look that could kill an owl.

Me and Frank read *Lady Chatterley's Lover* in an afternoon. We read the boring bits together and then when it got saucy he'd go outside and we'd take turns and pass it through the letterbox. When we finished we sat down on the couch and both thought the same thing – 'We can do better than that.' No, that's not right. I was thinking, 'I can do better than that,' and Frank was probably thinking, 'I wonder what Bob's thinking?'

I got a big pad and Frank's mum's typewriter and told Frank to leave me to write. A few hours later I'd done the first page of *Lord Dundee's Lover* and I was absolutely buzzing until Frank got back a bit sheepish and said he'd told the boys in Stewpot's what I was doing and he'd agreed that I would do a public recital that night and there was a lot of excitement. Worst of all was that he said Cruncher McKenzie was coming. Cruncher was not only one of the hardest nuts around he's also always been the biggest bookworm I know. He told me once that if I was to cut his arm he'd bleed Agatha Christie and, put it this way, if Cruncher McKenzie was expecting a recital then I had to give one.

I didn't even have time to give Frank into trouble properly for arranging the recital because I had to get my hair looking nice (which it always did back then – it was black as coal and twice as shiny) and finish off the page. Because it wasn't quite the full story I just made it end on a cliffhanger and then we headed to Stewpot's while I at least managed to give Frank into some trouble on the way.

There was a good crowd in Stewpot's and I was certainly excited when I stood up on the chair and started reading. All the boys were shouting out things like 'Here we go!' and 'It's looking good for Lord Dundee!' and 'Not long now!' But then I got to the cliffhanger, thanked them for their support and got down from the stool and I have to say the reaction was desperately disappointing. I wasn't necessarily

LORD DUNDEE'S LOVER

(by Robert Servant of Broughty Ferry, Dundee,
no copying allowed)

"Oh it's yourself", said Lord Dundee as he opened the
door. Lord Dundee was a handsome bastard of a man. Great
big muscles and nice hair and a good smile and teeth and
big muscles. He opened the door and in walked a very nice
woman indeed.

"Hello Lord Dundee my name is Victoria Magnolia" said the
woman. She was a fantastic woman in both looks and
figure. She had lovely long blonde hair like the sun and
nice eyes and there was nothing at all wrong with her
face and also her legs and you could see down her top a
bit but not in a bad way and there was nothing wrong with
the bit you could see.

"Well, well, well Victoria Magnolia", said Lord Dundee,
laughing in a way that showed he was not under any
pressure whatsoever. "Well, well, well".

"Oh Lord Dundee", said Lady Magnolia who was also a Lady
but not because she was married to Lord Dundee because
she wasn't. His wife had died in the War and her husband
was just a wee guy and anyway he didn't have any legs
because of the War also so it didn't matter. But he was
wee anyway even despite the legs situation and hardly a
patch on Lord Dundee who had long legs but in proportion.

"Well, well, well", said Lord Dundee and behind him was
all the heads of the deers and wolves that he'd killed
when he was hunting up in the Highlands around Inverness
and also in other parts of the Highlands. "You're a sight
for sore eyes Victoria Magnolia, I'll tell you that for
free".

Victoria Magnolia was a sight for sore eyes all right.
She was bloody gorgeous and she didn't take herself
seriously but that's not to say she was always telling
jokes. She laughed at Lord Dundee, not making fun of him
but in admiration and put her hand over her mouth as if
to say "Woops!"

"Well, well, well", said Lord Dundee and he said "Are you
looking for this" and he took off his gloves and hung
them on the head of one of the deers he had shot and then
he was ready and Victoria Magnolia thought "Oh oh" and
then there was a cliffhanger.

expecting a standing ovation, though it would have been nice to get one, but I certainly didn't expect what happened. Crusher looked at me for a long time then left, and the rest of them lost the plot.[34]

Stewpot smuggled me out the back door and it took a few weeks before people stopped giving me abuse in the street, mostly for being a 'bottler' and a 'tease' which was a lot of rubbish but it was enough to rob me of my confidence and force me to abandon *Lord Dundee's Lover* with immediate effect. But the boo boys can get you, there's no doubt about that. They get in your head and make you wonder who you really are. There's many times in my life that I wish that I'd stood up to them and *Lord Dundee's Lover* is very much one of them.[35]

---

34 See *The Dundee Courier*, 29 July 1967 – *'Police Called To "Cliffhanger" Riot* (Chaos reigned in a Broughty Ferry bar last night as a local man delivered an unexpected cliffhanger . . . "Totally out of order" . . . "Cheated" . . . "What gives him the right to play God?"')'.

35 I found the incomplete *Lord Dundee's Lover* and it is included opposite. I think, immodestly, that it is a great testament to my editing skills in this book, demonstrating as it does the raw material I have to work with.

15

Frank's Mum Going to
Live in the Nursing Home

Frank's mum going into the nursing home was a surprise to a lot of people but when people say, 'Why did Frank's mum go to live in a nursing home when she was 38?' I've always said the same thing, 'None of your business and don't be a boo boy.' The boo boys used to make jokes about it but that was one area I wouldn't let them make jokes about in front of Frank and I still won't. I don't mind them making jokes about his clothes or hair or the way he walks or his smile (which makes you want to cry) or his reading problems or his troubles with his laces or his stupid jokes or the time he got lost in his own house or the time I put those rocks in his garden and told him there had been a meteor storm and he stayed indoors for a week.

But I won't have jokes about Frank's mum and the fact she lives in a nursing home because she's a decent woman and, I'll tell you this for free, moving into the nursing home was the best thing she ever did. I know what the boo boys would say, that moving into a nursing home is hardly difficult if you've got the readies but they're talking bollocks because moving into a nursing home when you're 38 is a tough sell all round. Believe it or not it was all her idea.

Frank's mum always reminded me of an old-style football winger. She was funny-looking, had buckets of natural ability but was easily knocked off her game by the boo boys and when her confidence went she'd fold like a cheap suit. She was no Bobby Dazzler and the worse thing was that she knew it. She said she wasn't interested in other men out of respect for Frank's dad (I'm not sure if that was entirely her decision because, put it this way, Frank gets his looks from his mum but he looks like he should get his looks from his dad) but that didn't stop her saying things like 'Oh look at my silly hair' or 'Oh look at my daft clothes' or 'Oh look at my stupid son', and I used to say, 'Hey, come on, there's nothing wrong with your hair or your clothes,' but she wouldn't listen and she'd mope about for days on end.

Then one day Frank's mum came home and she was absolutely cock-a-hoop, singing to herself and giggling like a maniac over the mashed potato. She was like that again the next day and the next again day so Frank I asked what was up and she cracked and spilled the beans.

She'd gone to visit her aunt at the Goodbye And All The Very Best Nursing Home up in Stobswell. She reckoned it had been the best afternoon of her life. She said she might not have been the biggest cracker in the room but she was definitely in the top three, and that everyone there had listened to all her stories and jokes without a word of complaint. She said when she was leaving a couple of them clapped. Since then she'd gone up every day and she said that when she walked in they looked at her like she was Liz Taylor and Tommy Cooper rolled into one.

Frank and I were pleased to see her happy and it got her out the house but we didn't think much more of it until a couple of weeks later when she sat us down and said she wanted to move out the house and into the Goodbye And All The Very Best Nursing Home on a residential basis. She had Frank's dad pension to cover it and she said that the Nursing Home was her Everest as well as the only place she'd ever been where she felt that she was the bell[36] of the ball.

The next morning Frank's mum packed up her stuff and the three of us got a taxi to Stobswell. Frank was acting a bit strangely and his mum was nervous so I calmed everyone down with a few jokes and my Terry Thomas impression which they both lapped up and it wasn't exactly lost on the driver who nearly took out a cyclist he was laughing so much.

When we got there I sent Frank's mum to go and talk to her pals so the staff could see there wouldn't be any bust-ups and told Frank to wait outside. I asked for the matron and gave her the old big eyes and said I needed Frank's mum to move in. The matron was a tough nut to crack. She said Frank's mum was far too young and the other women would get jealous of her teeth and how quick she was on her feet.

---

36 Belle, presumably.

I pointed out that she'd be great advertising for the Nursing Home because people would see her and think there must be something in the water and stick their grannies in there as well.

She said that Frank's mum would likely be staying for a good while unlike the others and what if she was a disrupting influence and I said, 'Well would you call that a disrupting influence?' and pointed over and Frank's mum had told the other women in the Nursing Home a joke and they were all laughing like it was a belter (which to be fair it probably wasn't but that's not vital to the narrative).

The matron looked unsure and said that they couldn't really accept someone who was completely on the ball and I said that Frank's mum was a bit soft in the head and then, like a gift from God, Frank ran past the window doing an aeroplane impression. 'That's her son there,' I told her and did one of those faces that muggers use which says, 'I think you know what I'm saying and I would just leave it there with the questions if I was you.'

That was that. Frank's mum was into the Goodbye And All The Very Best Nursing Home. On the way back I asked Frank how he knew to do the aeroplane stuff at the window and he went all red and said he didn't know what I was talking about and to my immense credit I just left it there.

To this day, Frank's mum lives at the Goodbye And All The Very Best Nursing Home. Frank and I visit on alternate weeks and it's good having a wee chat with her and telling her what I've been up to. She's a wee bit doolally right enough but she's happy with it. Frank and I were talking about that the other day there and he said that he looks at her and he sometimes wishes that he was mad as well. To my immense credit I just left it there.

16

Having a Girlfriend

In 1969 The Great Skirt Hunt came to an end when I got myself a girlfriend. Her name was Daphne but she should have been called Catastrophe and not because that sounds a bit like Daphne but because that's what she was. She was a girl-next-door type. If you happen to live next door to a fucking idiot.

Believe it or not things started not too bad between me and Daphne before they got bad and then really bad with the hiding but it all looked so different that night I walked into the Limbo Dancing Club with Frank and said, 'Stop the bus, Frank, look at that one.' The Limbo Dancing Club was always a good way to meet skirt who were fun and fairly flexible and Daphne ticked both boxes. She was one of the best limbo dancers in Dundee at the time and when we started chatting it was like someone had taken magic dust and rubbed it into my mouth and her ears because everything I said she just cracked up and hung on my words like a puppy. 'This is looking good, Bob,' said Frank, before I told him to go and stand a bit further away.

From then on I was up at the Limbo Dancing Club most nights winding up my relationship with Daphne like a coiled spring. She would do a bit of limbo dancing with the other girls then come over and I'd make the same joke and she'd always laugh even though it was the same joke. It wasn't even a proper joke I'd just say that I thought she must be made of rubber. This was before I realised that she was mostly made of anger and, in the case of her heart, bricks.

The first few months having a girlfriend were fine. We'd spend time together and have a laugh and there was a fair amount of the good stuff and things were ticking along when she said that her mum was selling her house to move closer to Tom Jones and could she maybe stay with me for a bit? She knew that it was just me and Frank in the house and it kind of made sense so I said, 'Aye, why not?' without really thinking about the consequences.

The first one of the consequences that I didn't think about was Frank. He'd always been relatively polite to Daphne but he went ballistic about her moving in, saying it was supposed to be just the two of us and how we were supposed to be like Butch Cassidy and the Sundance Kid and all this. I said that I had never agreed that the two of us would be like Butch Cassidy and the Sundance Kid but I apologised for not checking in advance and asked him to just give Daphne a couple of weeks to see how it goes, which he reluctantly agreed to.

So in she came and oh dear right from the start it was hard work. Any time Daphne started speaking Frank would groan and say, 'Oh God, here she goes again.' Daphne kept asking if I was going to do anything and I could see her point, Frank was really annoying me and she could obviously see that, so one day I went up to Turnbull's Timber in Wellbank and bought a load of plywood.

I got it delivered when Frank was out at his cycling lesson and went straight to work. It only took me a couple of hours to halve the entire house, with a few problems. I thought it was only fair to give Frank half the living room and because my side of the house included the downstairs toilet I had to give Frank half the upstairs bathroom so he could have a toilet as well. The other issue was the plywood was only six feet high so didn't quite reach the ceiling and noise carried badly.

The next few days were hard work. I had Daphne in one ear asking why I didn't do a better job with halving the house like I'm a Champion Builder or something and in the other I had Frank. Every time he knew we were in the living room he'd be at the other side pretending to be having a party. He'd run around the room talking in different voices, chinking glasses and opening and closing the door and saying things like 'Oh, oh, here's trouble' and 'Yes, room for a small one' and 'Good afternoon your Honour'. I had that nonsense and Daphne's moaning and I'd sit there wishing the floor would open up and swallow me and then spit me out in Stewpot's.

Then there was the bathroom. Frank would hear me having a bath and nip into his half of the bathroom and get on the job. To this day I don't know how he did this, and I don't have any great wish to learn, but Frank seemed to be able to produce the most appalling results through there almost at will. I'd nearly pass out in the bath which could have been lethal (and hopefully brought a murder charge for him) and in the end had to have secret baths in the middle of the night which weren't as much fun as they sound.

In the end though Daphne became such a nightmare that Frank was irrelevant. I don't know what happened to her, it was the strangest thing. At first everything was all nice and relaxed and we just sort of mucked about but then she started behaving really oddly. She had this thing she would do when she'd insist I join in with stuff she did. If she went for a walk along the beach at sunset, or to the cinema on a Friday night, or to a restaurant on her birthday, then she'd really forcibly insist that I went with her. I presumed she'd read some scare stories about local crime rates and told her that she'd be safe enough doing these things by herself but she completely missed my point and started with the shouting and bawling.

That kind of behaviour started to creep into the house as well. If I was sitting in the lounge having a wee think then she'd come and sit beside me. Then I'd go outside and sit on the bench and have a wee think and she'd come and sit beside me. So I'd go into the kitchen and have a cup of tea and Lo And Behold she'd pop up there as well and, oh what a surprise, she'd like a cup of tea as well! I presumed that someone, probably Frank, had told her that the house was haunted so I sat her down and said that she didn't always have to be in the same part of the house as me because there weren't any ghosts. Again, I thought I was helping her out but the result was another Hiroshima of an argument.

After that, things got worse.

17

Hiding Not Being an Olympic Sport

If hiding had been an Olympic sport in 1969 then I'd have been part of the Hiding Team for the 1972 Munich Olympics or the Hitler Olympics as they were commonly called.[37] In fact I'd almost definitely have been the captain and you tell me if an Olympic team captain would not automatically become a local Hero. You just have a think and tell me that. Not that you should need to have a think about it because the answer is yes with a capital Y.

I suppose I always knew I had a bit of a talent for hiding, you always do know these things I think, but it was Daphne that drove me into developing that ability into top, international-class performances. At first the hiding was pretty standard stuff. I'd tuck in behind doors, 'accidentally' lock myself out the house, take a 'long time' tying my laces and so on. Then I stepped things up a gear – under the bed, in the airing cupboard beneath a pile of towels, in a ball behind the couch. These moves (which I don't for one minute claim to have invented) would usually buy me a few hours but then it would be sudden capture and the Earache.

In the end I was coming up with some unbelievable stuff that took a fair bit of planning but the results speak for themselves. I hollowed out the inside of Frank's mum's grandfather clock and holed up in there for an entire Sunday. It must have been gone midnight when my tummy rumbled and she nabbed me. I told her I was checking the time but, oh no, it was all 'inconsiderate' this and 'lunatic' that.

---

37 Bob's way off here. The Games commonly known as the Hitler Olympics were the Berlin Olympics of 1936. For Germany to have entitled the 1972 Munich Olympics as the Hitler Olympics would have been needlessly provocative.

The final straw was probably the best hiding plan that I or anyone else from the Dundee area has ever come up with. Frank cocked it up for me, if I needed to tell you that. Up to this point he'd been pretty useful with the hiding which of course he supported because it annoyed Daphne who he had unfairly taken to calling Daftie. If I needed him to help then he was allowed to come round to my half of the house, help out and then slip away before Daftie, sorry Daphne, caught him.

This particular plan was a cracker. There was an old armchair in the back room that no-one used so I took the cover off, brought it through to the lounge and got Frank to put it on top me. We worked out a way I could sit so that it looked like a normal chair but I was also facing the TV that I could see through peepholes and had a bit of a space on my lap for provisions. I made a big bag of sandwiches, got a bottle of whisky and got back into the chair. It was absolutely perfect and if it wasn't for Frank I'd have spent days pretending to be a chair with Daphne none the wiser.

Daphne was having a bath when we got set up and once I was in the chair I told Frank to go back to his side of the house. Now, I can't remember exactly what words I used but I can tell you what I didn't say. I didn't say 'improvise' which is what Frank maintains to this day I said. The idea that under any circumstances whatsoever I would ever tell Frank to improvise is laughable. The idea that I would tell him to improvise while I was disguised as a chair is the stuff of nightmares.

Frank went outside, waited five minutes while he 'got into character' and rang the bell. Daphne came downstairs and opened the door and Frank said that he'd forgotten his key and walked through to the living room. He pointed at the chair I was hidden inside and said, 'That's a lovely chair, Daphne.' She said, 'So it is, where's that come from?' Frank said, 'I don't know but it's a lovely chair and that's all it is it's just a lovely chair, there's nothing more to it than that.' Daphne said, 'Well why don't you sit on it if you like it so much?' and Frank said (I kid you fucking not), 'I can't sit on it because Bob's inside it.' There was this horrible silence and then I took a deep breath, threw off the chair cover, held up the sandwiches and the whisky and shouted, 'It's party time and I'm the Chairman!'

Bearing in mind I had about five seconds to prepare I think I did remarkably well to come up with 'It's party time and I'm the

Chairman' but for Daphne it was not only not a good line it was also enough for her to pack her bags, say something about me and Frank's state of minds that was completely out of order in my case, and leave the house forever.

It was a shame for her sake that Daphne was such a tough person to live with because I'd be surprised if she ever got someone that could put up with her. But more to the point I'd become one of the best hiders around and it was just my luck that this one of the few sports that the Olympics has never recognised. It's unbelievable – you get the people doing the funny walk and the bow and arrow and all that but when it comes to hiding it's a complete no-no.

Still, at least it wrapped things up with Daphne. Relationships never end well and I'm glad the two of us broke up in a way that we'd probably have both laughed at later, if we'd ever seen each other again. Frank and I decided to go out to celebrate and luckily we had a reason to do so. It was Terry Wogan's 32nd birthday. We'd both got heavily into Wogan by that point and Stewpot let us have one photo of him up in the pub which was a nice gesture and added a happy ending to what had been a tricky few months.

Wogan's 32nd Birthday[38]

---

38 Photo courtesy of Bob Servant's private collection, all rights reserved. Inscription on back of photograph reads: 'Wogan's 32nd Birthday, 3 August 1970. I lent Frank £2.'

18

Making Frank My Number Two

I've made some great decisions in my life, really top class. I've never worn a cardigan, I've never had a moustache and I got my double entendre phase out the way in the 1980s before every man and his dog started using them under John Major.[39] Entering the window-cleaning game was another very good decision. Making Frank my number two wasn't.

The window-cleaning game is a hard business full of tough nuts but everyone knew it was a licence to print free money. By 1970 Frank and I were sick of doing jobs here and there and having to cut down on luxuries to make sure we had the readies to spend in Stewpot's every day. We were looking for something bigger and better, and one day in the summer of 1970 we found it when Stewpot leant over the bar, something he's always excelled at, and asked if we'd heard about Safehands Riley.

Safehands Riley wasn't the biggest name in window cleaning – that was Buckets Bennett from Invergowrie – but he was an established figure and had a respectable little round which covered off West Ferry from Victoria Road to Dawson Park. I was on nodding terms with him and Frank knew him on a 'Hello' basis, and he had a reputation for being a decent man and not thinking he was Cliff Richard like a lot of the window-cleaning big guns.

---

39 See *The Dundee Courier*, 5 April 1986 – '*Local Man Banned From Broughty Greengrocer* ("He'd stand at the counter making comments about the vegetables and weeping with laughter")'. See the *Daily Express* 17 May 1991 – '*Major Pleasure Promised to Female Cabinet Members*'. See *The Times*, 16 November 1991 – '*Prime Minister Anticipates "Major Election"*'.

What Stewpot told us was remarkable. Safehands Riley had been attacked by a German Shepherd at a house in Strathearn Road and had completely lost his confidence to go to houses with enclosed gardens. West Ferry is full of big gaffs so that had pretty much taken Safehands out the game and now he was looking to offload his round and get into something that, as he put it, 'would let him see his grandchildren grow up'.

I found that surprising, particularly because Safehands didn't have any kids, but I also saw it as an opportunity so I said, 'Action time, Francis,' and me and Frank headed up to Safehands' house in Ellieslea Road. There was no answer at the door but we heard him shouting and went round the front. He was hiding out in an upstairs bedroom and in a terrible state, unshaven and speaking to us through a gap in the curtains.

He said that the whole thing had been a nightmare and all he remembered was a big set of teeth, a lot of barking and feeling trapped. Sharp as a tack I said, 'That sounds like when I had a girlfriend,' which eased the mood and Safehands said it was the first time he'd laughed since he got out the hospital because all he'd been doing was sleeping, taking medicine and trying not to think about German Shepherds. 'Sounds like when I had a girlfriend,' said Frank and I told him to go and wait in the street.

Safehands and I got down to business. He said he'd give me his list of clients, a ladder, a bucket and more sponges than I'd ever need for £500. For the next half an hour I played every trick in the book. First I told him to say the price again in exactly thirty seconds, ran over to his outside tap, filled my mouth with water and then spat it out in surprise when he said the price. Then I did the 'get really angry and ask why they're treating you like this' move. Then I did the 'I'm walking away, I'm walking away' and walk really slowly until they call you back. Then I did the Woe Is Me and pretend to cry one-two. By the end Safehands was on the ropes and wrapped up in my web of tricks. We met at £496 as long as I paid cash.

I had a week to get the money and I came up with the fairest way of raising it. Frank kicked up a bit of a fuss, as I knew he would, even though I pointed out that selling off most of the house's furniture would instantly double the size of the rooms and to double the size of the rooms in any other way would cost a fortune.

He was particularly difficult about his mum's antique piano but, like I told him, neither of us could play a note and his mum would have to have pretty long arms to bang out a tune seeing as she now lived in the Goodbye And All The Very Best Nursing Home in Stobswell. I opened the windows and said, 'Shall we see if she can reach the piano, Frank?' and did the cupping the ear thing and finally he crumbled and admitted I was right. He looked a bit down, so I cheered him up by telling him I had two big surprises for him later that day, which was a bit daft because I didn't have any surprises for him at all and he'd almost definitely have settled for one.

But you don't get to where I am in life without being quick on your feet, so once the furniture cowboys had come and picked up the gear and given me my £500 I told Frank to get his jacket on and took him down to Vissochi's Ices on the harbour. 'Are we going to Vissochi's, Bob, are we going to Vissochi's?' he kept asking and he nearly exploded when we arrived and I ordered him a treble scooper which he's not really supposed to have because of his excitement problem.

We went and sat on a bench and looked out over the harbour. I was having a great think, mostly about the window-cleaning round and how much money I would make, and then Frank interrupted it by asking me what his second surprise was. It must have been the view or the fresh air but I took a deep breath and said that he was going to be my number two on the window-cleaning round.

He didn't say anything so I turned round and I don't think I'd ever seen him so happy. He had this big smile. He looked a bit like he was going to cry, and he had ice cream all over his face. I looked at Frank, sitting there at the harbour while the sun set and the swans quacked away, and I thought to myself – 'Oh sweet Jesus what have I done?'

19

Frank's Falls

1970, 1971 and 1972 were big years for me. I learnt a lot about life, I learnt a lot about business and, believe it or not, I learnt new ways in which Frank was an idiot. Traditionally, Frank had shown himself to be an idiot with things to do with his mind and his mouth but he pulled out a whole new twist over those years by showing me that slapstick could be a bad thing.

I've always loved slapstick and I still do. If you were to walk past my house on a Saturday teatime you'd be forgiven for thinking Billy Connolly was giving me a one-to-one or Del Boy was in here doing the falling through the bar routine over and over again but in fact it's just me watching the famous television show *You've Been Framed*.

I'm not sure if you watch *You've Been Framed* but I'll tell you right now that I've been watching the telly for fifty years and there's not been a better show and that includes the Coronation and the Cuban Missile Crisis. If you've not seen the show, *You've Been Framed* is a collection of short documentaries when everything is fine to start with and people are laughing and talking to each other and the boy on the camera will shout 'Grab the rope' or 'Stand closer to the water' or 'Come on then, do something' and you're sitting watching the documentary and you know what's coming so you're already sort of giggling to yourself and then BANG! it's slapstick time.

There's a few storylines that crop up a lot. Sometimes one of the people in the documentary will fall into water. Sometimes they'll fall off their bike into a bush. Sometimes they'll be hit in the knackers by a ball thrown by a kid. Sometimes they'll be dancing with the bride and the bride's dress will fall down, and so on and so on. It doesn't really matter because it's nearly always a belter. In fact the only bit of *You've Been Framed* I don't like is when they sometimes show a collection of documentaries where it's two babies kissing and the audience gives it the 'Aaaahhh' routine. If I want to see people kissing I'd watch *Gone With The Wind* or *Blind Date* and I'd want them to be grown-ups at least.

My point is that I'm a slapstick fan and probably one of the biggest around. If I'm walking to Stewpot's and a kid cycles into a lamppost or some skirt decks it in her heels then I'll be doubled over for about ten minutes. One time I saw a guy trip over his dog's lead and fall into an industrial bin outside Safeways and I was laughing so much I had to go home and put myself to bed and really, really try to get it out my head because I was genuinely worried I was going to have a heart attack. For the next month I took the long way to Stewpot's because I was scared if I went past Safeways I'd suffer an aftershock.

So when me and Frank started the window-cleaning round and he spent the next three years performing slapstick you'd think I'd be happy. But I wasn't because it was a pain in the arse. He was damaging the equipment and it hardly filled our customers with confidence. I tried to help him. First I put a photo of Terry Wogan on the bucket to give him some company up there but then he started

The Wogan Bucket[40]

40 Photo courtesy of *The Dundee Courier, Rising Business Stars*, 19 July 1974.

talking to Wogan, lost what little concentration he had and down he came. Then he said it was just bad luck so I bought a so-called lucky wooden elephant off Gypsy Henderson but that just gave Frank someone else to talk to and Lo And Behold he was lying on the ground and giving it the Can't Feel My Feet stuff.

If I was to list Frank's falls between 1971 and 1973 then this book would be as big as a house. Well, probably not quite as big as mine but probably as big as yours. Anyway, the falls were mostly the same. I'd tell Frank not to fall off the ladder – he'd fall off the ladder, I'd take a photo for insurance purposes, that photo would somehow wind up in Stewpot's, Frank would go in the huff because the photo had wound up in Stewpot's, Frank would resign, Frank would ask for his job back, I'd tell Frank not to fall off the ladder, he'd fall off the ladder, etc, etc.

It was tough going but there were some good moments along the way. I've just been up to my attic and gone into my Frank Being An Idiot Box. Frank says I keep the stuff in that box to pull out and humiliate him which is just pathetic. Anyway, here's some of his best falls.

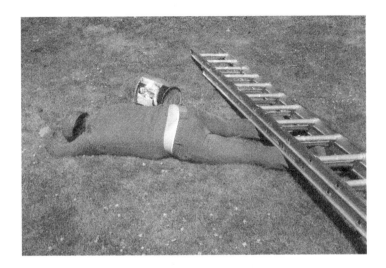

Incident Report[41]

Date – February 1971

Place – Bill Wood's garden on Strathearn Road

What Happened? – A nice soft landing for Frank's soft head. I'd left him up there talking to the Wogan bucket while Bill and I had a chat about a few political rumblings at the Bowling Club and then we heard this yell and, surprise surprise, there was Francis whimpering away.

Blame For Insurance Purposes – Frank

---

41 All four dramatic photos courtesy of Bob Servant's private collection, all rights reserved. In each case the inscription on the back of the photograph is the 'Incident Report' given.

Incident Report

Date – October 1972

Place – Dawson Park

What Happened? – We'd just won the contract for the Dawson Park greenhouses. Frank had taken to wearing a plastic helmet which in my view made him over-confident and that was proven here with gusto. This was probably my favourite of Frank's falls because of the way that just when he thought it was all over he got spanked by the ladder. It took me and the Parkies ten minutes to stop laughing, get a grip of ourselves and reluctantly lift the ladder off him.

Blame For Insurance Purposes – Frank

Incident Report

Date – August 1973

Place – The Taychreggan Hotel

What Happened? – This was embarrassing for several reasons. The Taychreggan was the biggest job on the round, Frank was left still holding Gypsy Henderson's so-called lucky elephant, he fell twice in one day, and he was wearing his Christmas jumper in the middle of summer. Under the circumstances it was hard to feel sorry for him and I didn't.

Blame For Insurance Purposes – Frank, Gypsy Henderson

20

Bringing Cruncher On Board

Even though some of them were decent entertainment I knew that Frank's falls had to finish. He was at risk of breaking the ladder and not all of our customers had as good a sense of humour as me and they played the Extremely Unprofessional and You're Sacked cards. I worked out that the only way I could guarantee that Frank would stop falling off the ladder was to get a real-life Strong Man to hold the ladder in a vice-like grip while I went off and charmed the customers with my eyes and stories.

The toughest nut I knew, of course, was Cruncher McKenzie, but he hadn't spoken to me since the *Lord Dundee's Lover* cliffhanger fiasco. I went to the shops and bought a copy of *Poetic Gems* by William McGonagall[42] and went up to his house.

Cruncher opened the door and did a look that could freeze a snowman. Then he saw the book and cracked the most wonderful smile and said 'In you come Robert'. We sat down in Cruncher's living room and he talked for about an hour about McGonagall and how he was much misunderstood and how Cruncher saw similarities with his own life.

'Was McGonagall a hard nut as well, Cruncher?' I asked and Cruncher looked very serious and said, 'Robert, he was the bravest man who ever held a pen.' I wanted to say 'What about Tony Hart?' so much it gave me a sore tummy but I bit my tongue and suggested that Cruncher came and worked with me and Frank on the windows.

---

42 William Topaz McGonagall, 1825–1902, much maligned Dundonian poet who suffered years of public humiliation in the bars of Dundee. Mercilessly lampooned by Spike Milligan through his McGoonagall character.

Cruncher said that he'd been working as a bouncer at the Goodbye And All The Very Best Nursing Home because they'd let in a young piece of skirt and all the old boys were thumping each other to try and impress her. I did a That's News To Me look and said working on the windows would get him out and about and Frank and I would happily talk books with him all day long. He had a wee think and then smiled again (not as good as the first time but by no means badly) and said, 'We few, we happy few, we band of brothers,' which I recognised as a lyric from an Elvis song. 'Just don't wear your Blue Suede Shoes, Cruncher,' I said and winked so he knew I was in on the joke but he didn't seem to want to keep it going.

Right from the start having Cruncher on the round was top class. He wore his donkey jacket and his Dundee United tammy hat and held the ladder in those big arms and my God I wouldn't have minded going up the ladder myself. Frank was cock-a-hoop and all in all it was a decent atmosphere other than the fact we had to listen to Cruncher talk about the common plot devices of Agatha Christie and how he wished Dick Francis would 'get over the horse thing' while Frank and I looked at each other with Just Agree With Anything He Says eyes.

One day I was berating Frank for all the customers we'd lost with his falls and Cruncher suggested I pay him a quid for every new customer he brought in. At the time it didn't seem a big deal but looking back it was like Jesus going to God and asking if there was anything he could do to help out. Just like Jesus was a breath of fresh air for the Christianity game, Cruncher's new customer search put me on the road to the business big time. Every day he'd have two or three more customers for us and the round got bigger and bigger.

Having said that, the customers Cruncher brought in were a funny bunch. They tended to be nervous individuals and most of them preferred to do their talking and paying through the letterbox but it was all the same to me. There was one guy who didn't even have any windows. He lived in a converted air raid shelter on Victoria Road but he left the money under the mat and shouted through the door to give his best wishes to Cruncher and suggested that we 'just check the roof if you have the time'. We didn't even bother doing that to be honest. Lord Lucan could have been on the boy's roof having a packed lunch and we'd already be fifty yards up the road.

The success of the round didn't go unnoticed and I got a call from

The Courier who wanted us to feature in their Rising Business Stars column.[43] These days I know what the press are like and they've put me through the ringer but back then I was blinded by the thought of getting in the paper and all the skirt seeing it so I said, 'OK then why not yes that's fine come down tomorrow.'

---

43 Photos on facing page courtesy of *The Dundee Courier*, all rights reserved. They show Cruncher McKenzie in his distinctive Dundee United woollen hat, Bob directing operations and Frank loyally perching on, or carrying, the ladder. The photos illustrated the *Rising Business Stars* section of 19 July 1974 – *'Skylights Are The Limit For Servant's Window-cleaning Round* ("We've got the most honest sponges in Dundee . . . We work hard and we play hard . . . I'd say to the other window cleaners reading this – pull your socks up because we've caught you with your pants down.")',

21

Frank Recruiting Halfwits Like Him

I got carried away with the Rising Business Stars article, there's no doubt about that. I shouldn't have challenged the rest of the window-cleaning community in print but when you're riding a wave it's very hard to stop rowing.

Sure enough Buckets Bennett came down to see me in his van. At first he was pretty angry giving it No Respect and so on but then Cruncher arrived and that took the wind out his sails a bit. In the end Buckets and I went for a walk in Dawson Park and did a deal. I wouldn't go west of the Kingsway dual carriageway and he wouldn't come east of it and in any future press interviews we'd speak positively of each other. I pretty much got everything I wanted and I went back to the boys feeling like Neville Chamberlain when he tricked Hitler into signing that confession.[44]

The result was that we could expand through half of Dundee and that's what we did. Cruncher kept bringing in the customers and Frank asked if he could recruit some other workers. He said he was supposed to be number two and he wanted more responsibility in the shape of being what he called 'a talent scout'. I agreed, which probably looks like a surprising decision, but you have to take into account just how good a manager I was.

When I read about some of the great Scottish football managers, I sometimes think I went down the wrong path in life. I'd love to sit down for a sherry and bacon roll with big Alex Ferguson and wee Jim McLean and have the three of us throw ideas and anecdotes

---

44 Due to time constraints, I'm going to stop correcting historical errors such as this. What's the point?

off each other like footballs. They are two men who understand the importance of man-management and it was the window-cleaning round where I first developed a lot of my talent in that particular area.

The most important thing in a window-cleaning round is morale and the ladders but a lot of the time morale is affected directly by the ladders. If there's a problem with the ladders then morale takes a dip and if everything's OK with the ladders then everything tends to be OK unless there's a problem with the buckets. Thinking about it, the buckets have an equal part to play in terms of morale along with the ladders. But if everything is OK with the ladders and the buckets then, generally speaking, it's only personal issues that bring problems, which is when you need man-management.

Some window-cleaners, like some footballers, need a firm hand and some window-cleaners, like some footballers, need the arm round the shoulder. If I saw someone struggling on the round then I would instantly make that call – a firm hand or an arm round the shoulder? Frank always got a firm hand. He knows himself, although he's never thanked me, that I made him the window-cleaner he became, which wasn't a very good one but it could have been a lot worse.

Nervous Norrie, on the other hand, was very much an arm-round-the-shoulder man. Norrie was the first guy that Frank came up with to join the team and I was understandably concerned. We both knew Norrie from Stewpot's, where he'd hardly covered himself with glory by hiding in the toilets for the Grand National despite the fact he didn't have a bet on, but Frank promised me the guy had his nerves under control.

A window-cleaner with nerves is pretty much the worst window-cleaner you can get because one of the great dangers on the round is someone opening the curtains when you're up a ladder doing the window. On the occasions I helped out on the ladders I didn't mind this at all because I saw it as a chance for a bit of a chat or, at the very least, some of the smiling and waving, but I was worried about Norrie. I take no pleasure in saying that I was spot on as always.

Norrie's window-cleaning Hiroshima came at a house in Duntrune Terrace. It belonged to Rash Scrimgeour, the deputy manager of Safeways who has that thing on his neck. Norrie was up his ladder when Rash pulled open his curtains. Norrie's never really spoken about what he saw but years later someone said something about

Rash Scrimgeour in Stewpot's and the thing on his neck and I heard Norrie whisper, 'Not just his neck,' in a really angry way.

Anyway, the result at the time was that Norrie screamed, fell off the ladder into a bush and hotfooted it down Duntrune Terrace towards the Claypotts shops. I ran after him to try and get the arm round his shoulder but he was running on fear and I'd have had more chance of catching Alan Wells. That was Nervous Norrie finished with the round. He did keep going to Safeways though, which never sat right with me.

After the Nervous Norrie disaster I told Frank he had to come up with something special. When he arrived with Titch Thompson I nearly knocked him out with the Wogan bucket. Titch Thompson came up to my belt but Frank said he'd be good for basement windows and skylights. I gave Titch a chance anyway and to be fair it wasn't bad having him around for the first few weeks. He was the quietest little guy you'd ever meet, never joined in the conversation and would only sometimes smile when me or Cruncher said a belter.

Then one day we were at some big house on Balmyle Road and it had a kid's Wendy House in the garden. 'Is that your house, Titch?' I said as a little joke to start the day and, my God, you've never seen anything like it. The guy went at me like a wild animal, grabbing the neck and so on. I saw the old white light coming for me until Cruncher got him off. Frank threw a bucket of water over Titch and then, oddly, a bucket over himself. Cruncher let Titch go and he ran off down the road. People go on about wee men and how they're always angry and want to wrestle the world but it wasn't till that day I realised just how unpredictable they could be.

I told Frank that he was sacked as talent scout and took on the hunt myself. I decided to spread the net a bit wider and put the word out in Monifieth which caused more internal problems. Frank said we should be providing Broughty Ferry jobs for Broughty Ferry people but I told him right there and then that when I see a good window-cleaner I just see a good window-cleaner and if everyone in the world thought like that we'd all be a lot happier.

I got four or five guys from Monifieth and they were all good workers. They liked coming to work in Broughty Ferry because of the improvement in air quality and they were able to buy electrical goods and Beatles records here and sell them back in Monifieth for twice the price. With the Monifieth boys slogging away, Cruncher keeping Frank on the ladder and me switching between firm hands and arms round the shoulders, things were on the up and up.

By 1978 we'd reached the Kingsway dual carriageway when we got the contract for Fyffe's Garage which is right in the middle of it. Just the other side of the traffic was Buckets Bennett. It was like the Kingsway was the Berlin Wall, Fyffe's Garage was Checkpoint Charlie, I was Franz Beckenbauer and Buckets Bennett was Daley Thompson.

Something had to give.

22

Selling Up to Buckets Bennett

1980 was a year for cool heads and big balls. Buckets Bennett and I were like two master chess champions, circling each other and sacrificing prawns[45] and sometimes going for little forays with our rooks and ladders. The thing was that we had great mutual respect. Sometimes we'd meet up on the forecourt of Fyffe's Garage for a pow-wow and it was always very relaxed. We'd talk buckets and sponges and then he'd suggest I backed off from the Kingsway and I'd suggest he did the same and we'd both look at each other for a long, long time and then we'd both walk away backwards.

I was never too worried because I had Cruncher McKenzie there and to be honest I was making so much cash I'd kind of lost my sense of fear. Every Friday I'd pay the boys then I'd go and stash what was left in the wardrobe at the bottom of my bed. I called it 'The Cupboard of Dreams', which I thought was a fun nickname but any skirt that came back to the house always seemed to get a bit edgy when I suggested they have a look inside.

By 1980 that wardrobe was the most valuable wardrobe in Scotland, and that includes any antiques that the Queen had through in Holyrood. The only way you could have had a more valuable wardrobe in Scotland in 1980 would have been to stuff one with Lulu and Sean Connery. Knowing Connery as I do[46] the big man wouldn't have a problem with that arrangement. He'd just look straight at the camera, send one eyebrow halfway to the moon, and slip into the wardrobe with that hairy chest of his twitching in the moonlight. And if I was Lulu, and I'm not,[47] I wouldn't be far behind.

---

45 Pawns, presumably
46 He doesn't.
47 He isn't.

With all the money I had stashed away in The Cupboard of Dreams I was living like a King. I had a wardrobe to be proud of and I ate magnificently. Great big steaks, lamb chops, whole sides of salmon. Poor old Frank would be sitting opposite grumbling into his sandwiches but, as I said to him, it was important he witnessed me eating like that because it gave him something to aim for.

So everything was moving along nicely when Cruncher arrived for work one day and made an absolute Chernobyl of an announcement. He had given up violence and was quitting the window-cleaning to start a small literary magazine called *Mumblings From The Margins* which would celebrate what he called 'the maverick and the forgotten'. I said he could celebrate the maverick and the forgotten working with me and Frank on the windows but he had made up his mind and I didn't fancy pushing him and finding out how committed he was to giving up the violence.

I had to act fast and I did. I begged Cruncher to work one last week, which he agreed to, then I went and tracked down Buckets Bennett. I told him that 'a man from Aberdeen' wanted to buy my round so I had just come to wish Buckets all the best. It worked a treat. He got angry and said after all our pow-wows he deserved the right to make an offer for my round. I said 'No bother, but the boy from Aberdeen is paying £17,400'. I only said £17,400 because Dundee United had just paid £17,400 for that Brazilian boy[48] and we'd all wondered if it was a funny number because of exchange rates.

Buckets gave the classic I'm Not Scared look more usually associated with washing machine repairmen and said he'd pay £17,401. I said, 'Buckets, you're a good man, you're a Dundee man, and you've got a deal.' The next day I went back with Cruncher and picked up the cash, had one of the best handshakes of my life with Buckets and went and found the boys.

I told them it was only the End of The Beginning and handed them all a month's wages even though none of them had a contract. That's the sort of man I am and they responded well. Cruncher said it would pay for the first issue of *Mumblings From The Margins*, the

---

48 See *The Dundee Courier*, 20 December 1979 – '*United Swoop For Samba Star* ("This is a dream for me. Growing up in las favelas our currency was dreams and the bravest dream I ever had was that one day I would play for Dundee United with Davie Dodds.")'.

Monifieth boys said they'd open a shop in Monifieth selling imported luxury brands and Frank said he was going to go and visit his cousin in Coupar Angus.

So that was that. The Bob Servant window-cleaning round passed into folklore, the team went off and did their own thing and I, well, I got myself into a bit of trouble.

23

The Gin Crisis

The Gin Crisis. My God, where to begin? Well, after I'd sold up to Buckets Bennett and paid off the boys I wasn't too sure what to do with myself. I thought I'd have a bit of time off, enjoy a couple of drinks and the next thing I knew I'd slipped into a living hell where it was just me, shouting, confusion and gin. It was a washout, a complete gin nightmare and I'm very lucky that I managed to claw my way out the other side.

I remember once watching Eric Clapton on *Wogan* when he talked about how hard he found it when a tour ended. He was used to life on the road when every day's an adventure and suddenly he had time on his hands and had to make his own sandwiches and brush his own hair and he got a sad feeling. I watched Clapton tell that story to Wogan and I smiled in that sympathetic way you get a lot from swimming pool lifeguards and said to the telly, 'I've been there, Eric, I've been right there.'

When I was one of the leading window-cleaning figures in Dundee I used to walk into Stewpot's and it was like someone had turned on a tap marked Respect. Boys would ask me how the round was going, and how many customers I was up to now, and if Frank had done anything funny that day. Skirt would be watching me out the corner of their eyes and giving me the Pretending Not To Care stuff and Stewpot would be wanting to talk to me at a businessman-to-businessman level.

But after I'd sold up I went in there and it was like a morgue. I got nods and hellos of course but nothing of any great substance and it was like someone had shaken all the magic dust out of my clothes and hair. I needed to gee myself up a bit, make myself feel like the big man again and unfortunately I found that in gin.

The great irony is that I knew the damage that gin could do. I'd seen Frank's aunt knit him jumpers with an extra arm. I'd read about the gin fan in Whitfield who strangled his neighbour's pet rabbit because he thought it was making withdrawals from his bank account and saying stuff about his wife.[49] I knew these stories and more and yet I still took a 9.5 double-pike swallow-dive into a great big puddle of gin and it took me a year to come up for air.

I remember the first gin I had very well, which is unusual. It was a particularly quiet afternoon in Stewpot's and I was getting absolutely nothing from anyone. Not even much in the way of gestures. I said to Stewpot, 'I think I'll try a gin please, Stewpot,' and he gave me one of those Oh Oh Here We Go looks so beloved by deep sea divers. He poured me the gin, I drank it and I'd found the answer to all my problems.

The Gin Crisis had begun. The afternoons weren't too bad. I'd be in Stewpot's delivering jokes and telling stories and although sometimes my words seemed to get their order mixed up, you could see that people were getting the gist of what I was saying from the way they looked at me. The evenings are a bit hazy. I remember something about a dog or wanting to be a dog but whatever it was I paid the money so no-one can point the finger on that one.[50]

After that, through no fault of my own, things slipped out of control. I can remember bits and pieces. Frank came back from his cousin's but said he didn't want to drink gin with me because of what happened to his aunt and I said that was selfish and we had a bust-up. Then I met some guy from Carnoustie on the bus and I told him about my bust-up with Frank and he said that he was a gin fan as well and he pointed down and I noticed that he had a bottle of gin with him on the bus and also that he was wearing one normal shoe and one welly.

I started seeing a lot of the gin fan from Carnoustie and then for some reason I was living with him. He had a small house in Carnoustie but from memory I was living in a tent in his garden which seems strange because it must have been yards from his

---

49 See *The Dundee Courier*, 6 June 1978 − '*Life's Not Funny For Whitfield Bunny*'.

50 See *The Dundee Courier*, 27 March 1980 − '*Broughty Ferry Terrorised by "Werewolf"* ', and *The Dundee Courier*, 28 March 1980 − '*Broughty Man Fined*'.

house and I've never been one for the camping. Apparently I was in Carnoustie for nine months which seems unlikely because these are my only memories –

Gin Crisis Memory One – Stewpot's Dad

Stewpot's dad has a Bed and Breakfast in Carnoustie and one day me and my pal had drunk all our gin and were going to buy more when we spotted Lee Harvey Oswald up on the roof of Stewpot's dad's place. We ran back to the house and the Carnoustie gin fan stole an air rifle from his neighbour's son then we rubbed mud into our faces and ran back to the Bed and Breakfast. Sure enough, there was Oswald, walking about up there like he owned the place and obviously hoping the Prime Minister or Idi Amin would drive past so he could sniper them.

We counted to three then stormed the Bed and Breakfast in a pincer movement. I shouted 'You've shot your last Political Big Shot, Oswald!' and my pal sprayed the Bed and Breakfast with the air rifle. Stewpot's dad came out and said something about the police and how the guy was a builder. I was worried he'd recognise me so I ran off and it took me a few hours to get back to my pal's house and the weird thing was we never spoke about Lee Harvey Oswald – we just had a singsong instead.

Gin Crisis Memory Two – The Pram

The two of us were charging through Carnoustie giving it the big one and then there was some issue with my leg and my gin pal found an old pram and he pushed me in it while we had a singsong and it was a decent atmosphere.

Gin Crisis Memory Three – Tom Baker, The End

I can't remember exactly what happened at the end between me and the Carnoustie gin fan but we were both very angry. He accused me of hiding gin and I accused him of being a liar and also that he was hiding gin. I got a bus back to Broughty Ferry and he tried to throw a brick at it but tripped over a wall and I fell asleep until someone woke me up at Dundee Bus Station.

The man that woke me up at the bus station looked exactly like Tom Baker. We got off the bus and I walked beside him saying that he looked like Tom Baker but then he started running even though he wasn't dressed for it. I ran with him for a bit to keep him company but I couldn't keep up so I stopped at a pub and they let me use their phone to call Frank.

The next thing I remember was waking up in my bed at Frank's and he was saying that he'd poured out all the gin and Stewpot wasn't going to serve me any either. Obviously I went straight for his neck but he'd tied my hands to the side of the bed using United scarves, which was unusually quick thinking from Frank.

For the next few days he fed me sandwiches and gave me tea through a straw. Once I'd got back my strength and my marbles he finally untied me and I got on with the job of piecing my life back together. When he talks about it now Frank always says that I came back from Carnoustie looking like I'd been in the Falklands and I say I wish I had been in the Falklands because at least then I'd have come home with a medal and God only knows I deserved one.

24

Mum Having to Cough It for Me to Get My Dream House

It took a wee while to properly get over The Gin Crisis. I told Frank not to start any singsongs because they'd become completely wrapped up in my mind with gin, and I stayed out of Stewpots for five long days. After that I pushed on and I'm very proud of the fact that I got over The Gin Crisis by myself. Not that it was rocket science. I'm sure most doctors would say the same to anyone suffering from a Gin Crisis – have a few beers and try to forget about it. Especially if we're talking about that doctor on the Perth Road that got busted last year.[51]

The most remarkable thing about The Gin Crisis was that I had some money left at the end of it, which isn't so much testimony to my budgeting but more that the guy from Carnoustie had been too drunk to ever charge me rent, though what the going rate is for sitting in a tent and drinking gin all day God only knows.

It was also testimony to Frank's honesty I suppose, though he'd always been intimidated by The Cupboard Of Dreams and worried that he'd be blinded by the riches. Either way, I was still nervous opening The Cupboard of Dreams but when I did there was a very decent pile there and I suggested to Frank that I should probably use the money to get somewhere of my own to live. He was a wee bit

---

51 See *The Dundee Courier*, Saturday 28 March 2009 – '*Perth Road GP Running "Nightclub" in Surgery* ("I went in for my bunions," says Cathy Instrell (56), "he told me to dance them off" . . . "I told him I was suicidal," says Jack Godden (62), and all he said was, "No frowns in Happy Hour" and then he tried to get me on his shoulders.")'.

funny about it but I pointed out that we were both in our thirties and it must be starting to look a wee bit odd that we still lived together and that could be the reason we hadn't had much skirt recently. He pointed out that The Gin Crisis probably had something to do with it, along with the fact he'd spent most days looking for me, which made me feel sad because I didn't realise he'd done that. So as a reward I didn't give him into trouble for bringing up The Gin Crisis when it was still so raw.

I started looking for somewhere to live and it was a disappointing experience. I suppose I was a bit spoilt living in Frank's mum's big house and the only places I could afford on my own were tiny little places that didn't have room for my clothes or my personality and certainly not both. Then the house next to Frank's went up for sale and it was an absolute cracker with a big garden and a view right up the river. Frank kept asking why I didn't buy that house because he thought it was funny that I wasn't able to buy it even though it was pretty much a direct match to my level of ability.

Things weren't looking too clever and they jumped off the cliff altogether when Uncle Harry phoned from Australia to say that Mum had died. It was a bit hard to get a full grip on the details because he was calling from overseas and had the TV up quite loud at his end but he said she'd passed away a few weeks before. Even though I hadn't seen Mum for over twenty years I was shaken up and asked about the funeral plans and he said, 'Oh I wouldn't lose any sleep over the funeral, you didn't miss anything there,' and how it was 'really boring'.

That hit me hard and I asked if she'd said anything about me before she died, even it was just a titbit or a throwaway remark. Uncle Harry said definitely not but there was a time a few years before when they'd been driving in the Outback and they'd seen some little kangaroo and Mum had said that it had reminded her of me. I'm not too proud to say hearing that Mum compared me to a beautiful boy kangaroo while on her deathbed made me feel a bit fizzy and I told Uncle Harry I needed to go but he said he was actually calling about something 'genuinely important'.

He said there'd been a mix-up with the will. They'd never sold the house in Broughty Ferry and Mum's will said it was to go to me. He said that clearly she'd made a mistake because she liked him a lot more than she liked me and therefore could I sign it over to him?

Hearing that Mum had left me the house as a 'sorry for not taking you to Australia and by the way you were always my favourite' gesture was one of the best moments of my life. I told Uncle Harry to fuck off, which was a pretty good moment as well, hung up the phone and headed up to the solicitor Pop Wood who dealt with Mum and Dad's divorce. He went through her file and confirmed the house was mine and the two of us went to see it. The house was in pretty good nick (later I found out Uncle Harry's brother had been living there on a sweetcorn[52] rent) and I told Pop Wood to stick it on the market without delay.

I didn't want to move back into the house because my memories of the place were kind of a mixed bag, plus I had a plan. A few weeks later I sold the house and the next day I swooped like a champion prize-winning kestrel and bought the house next to Frank's. You should have seen his face when I told him. He looked like he'd been kicked in the balls by Eric Bristow.

Moving into the house next to Frank's was absolutely marvellous. Thirty years later I'm sitting writing these words in that same house while the boy Forsyth wears my clothes and eats all my food.[53] These days the house is called Bob's Palace because of the work I had done with the cheeseburger money but even back when I first moved in it was a cracking gaff.

It's just a shame that Mum had to cough it for me to get my dream pad. Suddenly I was the last of the Broughty Ferry Servants and in tribute to her and Dad I decided I had to take the Servant name and drag it kicking and screaming into the big time. My opportunity was just about to arrive.

(That's a cliffhanger.)

---

52 Peppercorn, presumably.

53 Nonsense. I've never worn any of Bob's clothes and while staying with him I bought all the groceries in lieu of rent. And, seeing as he's brought it up, I don't think he'd find many people willing to meet a grocery list that regularly included household necessities such as book tokens, garden furniture and pornography.

25

The First Day of the
Cheeseburger Wars

People sometimes ask me when the Cheeseburger Wars started and
I always say the same thing. 'Slow down, wait, take it easy and just
fucking hold on a minute,' because there's something that needs to
be understood before we even start talking Cheeseburger Wars. First,
you have to know something about this city we call Dundee.

Dundee is a fish-and-chips city. Always has been, always will be.
Yes, we've had the odd fad. Bengali Bertie's back in the sixties, Right
Down To Chinatown up in the High Street these days,[54] and I'll hold
my hands up and say I've had a few pizzas in my time. But overall
it's fish this and chips that and that's what the people want. It's been
like that for hundreds of years and yet, for eight years in the 1980s
something peculiar happened in Dundee and Yours Truly was right
there in the middle of the action.

I'd heard whispers about a couple of vans that were floating about
the city centre selling American food, so Frank and I jumped on a
bus to see what the fuss was about. We found one of the vans down
in Dock Street and, my God, what a sight! 'Look at all these people,
Bob,' said Frank, and it was a fair point. If the crowd was impressive
that was nothing compared to what waited for us when we got nearer
the van and saw they were selling cheeseburgers.

Looking back it seems a bit daft that we were so impressed by a van
selling cheeseburgers, but you have to understand this was a different
time. We'd only ever seen cheeseburgers in American movies and

---

54 See *The Dundee Courier*, 26 June 2008 – *'Mao's About That Then?* ("I felt like
I was on the Orient Express," said Dorothy Chambers. 92.)'.

the idea that something from the American movies would wind up in Dundee was just ridiculous. It's not like King Kong had done his Look At Me stuff on top of the Law Hill or Godzilla had emerged from the River Tay and said, 'Hello Boys,' so why would Frank and I expect to see a van handing out American cheeseburgers in Dock Street at two o'clock in the afternoon?

I'm not a God man, just ask Father O'Neill, but being in the middle of that crowd in front of the cheeseburger van felt a bit like some Big Shot in the sky was reaching down and tapping me on the head and saying 'Pay Attention'. Frank pointed at one of the cheeseburgers and said, 'I'll have one of what he's having,' and I pointed at the van and said, 'No, Frank, we'll have one of what he's having.' It was a decent line. It didn't make perfect sense but the message was there.

Frank and I got the bus back to the Ferry and I cracked open the classifieds. There it was. An old ice cream van up in Douglas, £200 the lot. I was so excited I sprung for a taxi for me and Frank, and half an hour later, in the garden of a house in Douglas, I saw my Everest. It was rusty, dented and needed a paint job. If it was a woman it would have been put down, but for me I just saw bags upon bags of raw potential.

'My eyes have seen the glory, Francis,' I said and he asked me if I was back on the gin. I said that was both hurtful and wrong and he should pay attention because this was a Eureka moment just like when the apple fell on the boy's head and Stephen Hawking built the first-ever computer.

The guy who owned the van said if we'd finished talking bollocks would I like to take it or not. I gave him a smile that said Oh If You Only Knew and handed over the £200. That, right there, was the beginning of what is known today as The Cheeseburger Wars.[55]

---

55 See *Dundee 1982–89, A Time Of Change, A Time of Rebellion* (Edinburgh University Press, 2003) by Professor James Walker. ('What began as a welcome spread of provincial entrepreneurship would in turn feed a mania comparable to the European witch craze of the 1600s. Like then, a people would be first radicalised and then seemingly possessed. Local governance would be engulfed and compromised, societal rules and normality would be abandoned, and victory would belong to the corrupting and the corrupted. For Dundee, a small northern European city, this meant enduring a collective insanity for eight long years while the rest of Britain studiously ignored the city's plight. Pop concerts would be held for Africa, a war would be fought for faraway islands and yet in our midst a city was being strangled by hubris and the unquenchable thirst of the new. Who wept for Dundee? Only Dundee and that is the tragedy.')

Bob and Francis at the van[56]

26

People Talking About the Wild West But Forgetting About the Quicksand

Sometimes in life success creeps up on you. Sometimes you wake up in the morning and it's sitting naked in a chair watching you and saying, 'Nice sleep?' That's what happened with me and The Cheeseburger Wars.

Things moved fast from the start. I told Frank to get the van ready while I went and struck up relationships with butchers, bakers and the notoriously hard-to-please vegetable mob that were based on fair prices and mutual respect. At night Frank and I would watch American movies with Frank's finger poised like a Harrier jet over the pause button on the Betamax. When a cheeseburger came on the screen I'd shout, 'Pause the Betamax!' Frank would slam his finger down and we'd both go and sit right in front of the telly and let the image of the cheeseburger burn into our minds. Frank complained that when he closed his eyes at night all he saw was cheeseburgers and I told him that was exactly what I wanted to hear.

I'll never forget the first day we took the van out. The van ran on petrol, the fryer ran on gas and Frank and I ran on pure adrenaline. Who wouldn't when they were operating a cheeseburger van without a licence? The cheeseburger scene had caught the council on the hop and they were still trying to work out the licensing situation but Frank and I just couldn't wait any longer. Not when there was a killing to be made.

I'm often said to be the first cheeseburger van operator in Dundee. As I've already told you, that's not true. I was the best, there's no doubt about that, but I reckon we were probably the fifth cheeseburger van in Dundee. That's the fifth van on the road when there were already around 10,000 confirmed cheeseburger fans in the city. It was like shooting lions in a barrel and that's exactly what we did.

It seems strange considering what was to come but in those early days there was a great atmosphere between the cheeseburger pioneers, a real community spirit. We were similar to fishermen meeting up on the High Seas to tell each other where the best catches were and give each other tattoos.

Once you knew where that day's cheeseburger hotspots were you'd go down there, turn on the fryer and within ten minutes it was like the last bus out of Saigon. I was earning a fortune and as soon as I had enough in The Cupboard Of Dreams I started expanding. Every time an ice-cream van popped up in the classifieds I'd swoop like a peregrine falcon and snap it up.

Luckily for me (but not for them) the luxury goods shop that the Monifieth boys had opened had gone bust because of the arrival of the Argos catalogue, so they were quick to jump on board. I set them up with a couple of vans and handed them a map of Dundee. They asked where they should go and I said that they should be like dentists – keep the equipment clean, wash their hands and look for open mouths. There were no rules, you see, and that was how we wanted it. The city hadn't been carved up like with the window-cleaning and we could just set out in the van and see where fate took us.

One day I was answering Frank's questions about the situation and I said that it was like the Wild West. A few days later we were at the Claypotts roundabout when one of the other van owners pulled up. They started chatting to Frank and talking about how busy they'd been and Frank said that it was like the Wild West.

Traditionally I pull Frank up if he uses one of my jokes because he instantly cheapens the material by doing so but in this case I let it go. Within days I'd heard half a dozen van owners trotting out the Wild West line and smiling like they were Les Dawson. One of the Monifieth boys even used it to me and to my great credit I let that go as well.

The problem wasn't that my joke of Dundee being like the Wild West had been stolen and used without the slightest nod in my direction. The problem was that it really was like the Wild West in Dundee back then and everyone seemed to have forgotten what the Wild West was like. I've been a cowboy nut right from my Lone

Ranger days and I probably know more about the Wild West than anyone in Dundee.

Yes, there were saloons and singsongs and card games and flinging women across your saddle and all the rest. But there were also shootouts, ambushes, lynching and quicksand. And that's what people seemed to forget. They thought the Wild West was a bed of roses. I saw all the different cheeseburger van owners laughing about the Wild West at traffic lights and I used to shake my head and think 'What about the quicksand?' Once again, I was to be proved right.

27

The Failure of the Bank of Scotland's Executive Winners Club

Two years into the Cheeseburger Wars I'd made more money than I'd ever seen. How much? Don't be tacky, but let me say this. There wasn't a gameshow on the telly where the top prize was higher than what was in The Cupboard of Dreams. I used to watch those gameshows and they'd win the top prize and give it the Just Can't Believe it and Wildest Dreams stuff and, although I'd be more than happy for them, it was hard for me not to shake my head, waggle my finger, cross my legs and think 'small time'.

I could have hosted my own gameshow in the house with The Cupboard of Dreams as the star prize although, to be fair, I'd only have done it if the television channel who broadcasted the show would replace the money in The Cupboard of Dreams if the contestant won. Otherwise there would have been no financial benefit in me hosting the show plus I would have had to put up with a lot of strangers in my house and chances are that at least a few of them would be fannies.

Anyway, my point is that I was rolling in cash and wondering what to do with it when I found myself wandering down Humperdinck Avenue[57] past the Bank of Scotland. In the window was a poster saying, 'Ask Today About Our Executive Club'. Worth a couple of minutes, I thought to myself, and went and asked for the manager in that ultra-confident way that I handle myself in banks and at christenings.

Sometimes when you meet someone you can tell straight away that they're going to need a hand. Some people call it bullying but that's

---

57 See *The Dundee Courier*, 3 August 1972 – '*Singer "Surprised and Honoured" By City Gesture*'.

not true. It's about giving people a hand by helping them and making them do things that you tell them because it's for their own good. The manager at the Bank of Scotland was one of that mob. He was a weedy wee guy, very nervy and he could barely get his words out.

He told me that the Executive Club was a new type of bank account where you got a leather cover for your account book and a fountain pen. I told the manager that wasn't a bad start but if he wanted to impress the local business community he was going to have to come up with a bit more. He asked what I suggested and I told him to meet me at the bank the next morning an hour before opening. He said that sounded like a security risk and I said the only risk to his security would be if he didn't turn up and gave him a look that could bend steel.

That night was Wogan's 47th birthday and we celebrated it in style but even then I rolled up early the next morning and was pleased to find the manager waiting for me. He opened up and I had a good look at the bank's reception. To the side of the counters was a door. I asked the manager what it was and he said, 'Stationery.' Now, I said, ask me what's in there. 'What's in there?' he asked. 'Opportunity,' I told him.

I told the manager that I was a major local business success story and if he gave me permission I could get a hundred local Big Business Wigs signed up the Executive Club. He started on about bank procedure and I took off my jacket. I'd worn one of Frank's nephew's t-shirts so it was tight over my muscles. With the fingers of my left hand I did the Slow Caterpillar routine up my right bicep and looked him in the eye and whispered, 'Do you eat meat?' He folded like a pack of cards and said I could have that day as a trial run.

The first thing I did was rename the Executive Club as The Executive Winners Club to make it punchier. The manager went off to change the forms and I found a marker pen and wrote 'The Winner's Enclosure' above the stationery cupboard door. He grumbled a bit about that but the bank was opening so he gave me the forms and left me to it.

Straight away I started working the crowd and showing them the forms and asking them if they'd like to come into The Winners Enclosure. It was tough going. The most common reasons people gave for not joining me in The Winners Enclosure were that they were happy enough with the bank account they had, or they didn't like how small my t-shirt was or that they knew for a fact that The Winners Enclosure was the bank's stationery cupboard. When you're faced with narrow minds like that a lot of people would have given up but I kept going and finally I got a few people to at least join me in The Winners Enclosure for a chat.

Unfortunately there were a couple of problems with The Winners Enclosure that the manager had failed to tell me. It was too small to have seats in it so the customer and I had to stand quite close to each other. And there wasn't a light. Because I was having confidential discussions I obviously had to close the door and some of the customers just didn't have the confidence in themselves to handle the overall situation.

What with all the screaming the manager started to really let himself down, saying how my trial was over and I had to go. Needless to say he was too scared to come out from behind the glass so I hit back by trying to steal the pens but they were on chains and I ended up having a glorified tug-of-war with the pen holders which wasn't how I wanted things to end but it was the manager's fault that it did so. Either way, I got one of the pens off eventually, held it up and snapped it in two to show him it was a Metaphor, and then walked out the bank with my head held high.

Looking back, it's a shame that the manager fucked up the Executive Winners Club. I'd like it to have succeeded not for the glory, although that would have come in spades, but for the fact that it would probably have been good for me to have had a bank account.

You see the thing about my money is that I've never really paid any Kriss Akabusi. I've always meant to pay Kriss Akabusi, I mean it's not like I don't use the streetlights and I suppose the Army keeps me as safe as anyone else, but I never paid any Kriss Akabusi on the window-cleaning money so I just never bothered paying any Kriss Akabusi on the cheeseburger money either. But the way I see it is that, yes, maybe I've not paid as much Kriss Akabusi over the years as I could have done, but I've also given a lot of other people jobs. I'm sure some of them will have paid at least a little bit of Kriss Akabusi so that's something I can throw back at the Kriss Akabusi boo boys. [58]

---

[58] You may notice this last paragraph reads a little strangely. I have substituted the name of the British athlete Kriss Akabusi for a word that, if left unaltered in the copy, could have seen Bob prosecuted by the relevant national authority.

Wogan's 47th Birthday[59]

28

The Cheeseburger Civil War

The Cheeseburger Wars came in two parts. There was The Cheeseburger Civil War and The Cheeseburger World War, but the important thing to remember about both is that there wasn't any fighting. Not a single punch, not one karate chop. They weren't like the wars you get in books or in the Top Ten Wars lists that it's fashionable to talk about at parties. The Cheeseburger Wars were fought using words. Words became bullets and people's mouths became guns.

The Cheeseburger Civil War was a war of rumours and it all started, surprise surprise, because of money. By 1986 Dundee had finally reached its limit for cheeseburger vans. Every man and his dog had entered the trade and suddenly things got very tense. The relationship between van owners became like a failing marriage. You don't trust them, you stop talking to them and you start to stockpile mince reserves. If we saw another van at the traffic lights we'd look straight ahead, if we bumped into one at the garage we'd pretend to read the paper and if we overtook one on the Kingsway dual carriageway we'd close our eyes until we were past which was dangerous but saved embarrassment.

What I call The Great Silence only lived for a few months before it was drowned by The Rumours. No-one knows where and when The Rumours started but the first time I was aware of them was one day when Frank and I had parked up at Baxter Park next to the Rock Hudson statue[60] and a friend of Frank's came over and asked if we had

---

60 See *The Dundee Courier*, 19 September 1968 – '*Actor "Startled" By News Of Statue*'.

anything other than monkey meat. Frank said he wasn't sure (because he's a tool) and I asked the guy what he was talking about.

He said he'd heard a rumour we only sold monkey burgers. Frank's pals are often soft in the head, he meets most of them at adult swimming lessons, so I didn't take much notice until later that day when a woman in Commercial Street called me the 'Pol Pot of the monkey world' and a couple of kids in Kolacz Crescent asked if we were 'the Tarzan van'.

From there The Rumours were just ridiculous. There was the one about our Limeade being stolen from a children's home, that stuff about us being diehard Idi Amin fans (I'd followed the guy's career but I'd never been an out-and-out fan) and then all the nonsense about me having a false neck. I never understood how having a false neck would affect the quality of my cheeseburgers but you can't debate with these people. And anyway I didn't have a false neck. And I still don't.[61]

I knew The Rumours were coming from the other van owners but it was impossible to track down the culprits. I had to act and I did what any self-respecting local businessman does when he finds himself in a sticky spot. I bribed councillors.

Dundee City Council had finally set up a Cheeseburger Van Licensing Committee in an attempt to get some control over the situation and I found out the names of the three councillors that sat on it. They were Tuck Cummings, Gripper Wright, and Swapper Coley and as soon as I had their names I went to work.

The thing about corruption is you have to get inside the mind of the person you're corrupting and then pull his or her levers as if they're a forklift. The first forklift I had in my sights was Tuck Cummings and I was in a strong position because he was a notorious cheeseburger fan. At first I did the Pretend To Be Passing By routine when he got home at night and gave it 'Oh Councillor Cummings come and have a cheeseburger'. Then I'd 'forget' to ask for his 'money' and soon he was having a 'free' burger every day.

I let it go for a week then gave him a cheeseburger and a bill for nearly twenty pounds. He was furious and said he thought I'd been giving him the burgers for free. I said 'Why would I?' He said 'Because I'm on the Cheeseburger Van Licensing Committee.' I said

---

61 He doesn't.

'I like the way you're thinking,' and took back the bill and we looked at each other for a long time (but not in a saucy way) and slap, bang, wallop, he was in my pocket.

With Gripper Wright it was about identifying his weak spot which, as anyone in Dundee could have told you, was monkey bars. Like anyone who has lived a little knows, monkey bars are the heroin of the playground and Gripper had got hooked at an early age. He'd had some recognition[62] for his swinging before age caught up with him and he'd gone into politics instead.

Dundee's monkey-bar scene centres round the Dawson Park bars which for local swingers are like Hampden Park and Dunkirk rolled into one. They're so popular that weekends are Kids Only but when Frank and I found out Gripper lives round the corner from Dawson Park our ears pricked up like rabbits.

Early that Saturday morning we went and holed up in the bushes beside the tennis courts. Those bushes give a grandstand view of the monkey bars but Frank was annoying me by saying stuff as if he was in the Army and I was just about to call the whole thing off when Lo And Behold we saw Gripper Wright skulk through the gate. He had a quick look about then let out the most magnificent scream (later agreed by me and Frank to sound like a Red Indian) and ran at the bars. It was a wonderful sight and we gave him a few minutes out of respect for the performance then crawled out the bushes and walked over. 'Having a good time up there, Gripper?' I asked and slap, bang, wallop, he was in my other pocket.

That was two councillors down but I hit a problem with Swapper Coley. The guy was a real Goody Two-Shoes, even all the swapping he did was for charity,[63] so I knew I was going to have to come up with something special. Frank and I tailed him home from the council and the one thing I noticed was how cold he looked. It was getting into winter and the guy didn't have a big coat on. If someone doesn't wear a big coat in winter they're either mad, a hard nut or in between big coats. Swapper wasn't a hard nut (you could tell by his walking style

---

62 See *The Dundee Courier* 30 June 1964 – '*Local Monkey Bar Youngster "Could Go All The Way"* ("He's Spiderman without the arrogance," says Arthur Justice, Fixture Secretary of the "Broughty Swingers").)'.

63 See *The Dundee Courier* 2 November 1984 – '*Dundee Man Donates Annual Swapping Windfall to Charity* ("It's something I've always done," says Coley. "It's just a case of asking about and believing in yourself.")'.

which was pretty desperate stuff) and he wouldn't have been allowed to work on the council if he was mad, so I had my way in.

The next day Frank and I went up to Debenhams. We went to the Big Coats department and saw there was only one duffel coat left so I distracted the girls with a story about Gavin Hastings while Frank nicked the duffel and slipped away. I asked the girls if they had any decent duffel and they said that there was one left and we all walked over and then they started with the Hands Over The Mouth and Lock The Doors There's Been A Robbery stuff and I was giving it Eyebrows Up and What's All This About material in return.

Sure enough it made the paper[64] and we gave it a few days to calm down then went and laid the duffel on Swapper's doorstep with a note saying it was from 'An Admirer'. We hid in a bush and took photos of him trying it on and looking all pleased with himself. For the next week we kept an eye on Swapper and you should have seen the guy, showing off to the neighbours and stopping for chats just so he could get a compliment on the duffel.

Swapper Coley[65]

---

64 See *The Dundee Courier*, 26 November 1986 – *'Duffel Coat "Opportunist" Hunted'*.
65 Photo courtesy of Bob Servant's private collection, all rights reserved. Inscription on back of photograph reads: 'Stitching up Swapper Coley with the stolen duffel'.

After the week was up I put him out his misery. I waited till he was halfway up his path then stormed up behind him like Roger Cook and gave it, 'Having a good time in the duffel councillor, having a good time in the duffel?' He was all cocky and said that yes, he was having a good time and I was welcome to feel the material if I was another duffel fan. I took out the newspaper article about the theft and the photos of him wearing the duffel and held them in his face. 'Touché,' I said, which later I regretted as it would have been better to say, 'Game, set and match.' Either way, I had Swapper Coley by the balls.

With the Cheeseburger Van Licensing Committee under my control I soon put an end to The Rumours by having the licence revoked of any van owner that I didn't trust. The message got through – Bob Servant was in charge and he wasn't in the mood for jokes unless they were his jokes. With fewer vans on the road everyone was happy. Van owners were talking to each other again and there were plenty of punters to go round. The Cheeseburger Civil War was over but I barely had time to draw breath before the arrival of The Cheeseburger World War. It was like getting the better of Chris Eubank, walking round the corner and being clotheslined by Frank Bruno.

29

The Cheeseburger World War

The Cheeseburger World War was fought between Dundee's Cheeseburger Community and the Rest of The World. It was like David against Goliath's Dad and the worst thing was that it was the local paper that kicked the whole thing off. Up until 1988 *The Courier* had stayed on the sidelines with relation to the cheeseburger scene because they knew a lot of their readers were committed cheeseburger fans. But suddenly a few bits and pieces began to pop up in the paper. There would be a story about falling health rates or rising burglaries and I felt like a scientist standing at the top of a volcano with all the tourists taking photos but I'm looking at a little plume of smoke and whispering, 'Oh Sweet Jesus it's party time.'

Sure enough one morning I woke up to Frank banging on the door like a lunatic and shouting, 'They've come for us, Bob, the bastards have come for us!' *The Courier* had done a splash and it wasn't pretty reading.[66] Over the following weeks all sorts of jokers and Big Shots started arriving in Dundee. National newspapers, TV cameras, photographers, they all showed up. You'd think the Nuremberg Trials had been moved to Dundee Sheriff Court and the media chased us van owners about like hyenas.

I sent out word to the other van owners and we met in Dawson Park for a pow-wow. There was a lot of squabbling and I let them tire out then nodded to Frank and he called for silence. I stood on a crate and started to speak. Over the years people have talked a lot about what

---

66 See pages 1–14 of *The Dundee Courier*, 19 July 1988 – '*The Courier Takes a Stand.* (Cheeseburger Catastrophe . . . obesity levels . . . mass truancy . . . the return of scurvy . . . a once proud city . . . laughing stock of the world.)'.

I said that day in Dawson Park and I've got my own opinions. I've heard the Churchill comparisons and the stuff about Wogan, although personally I don't think Wogan would have thrived in that situation because it was too serious. Others call it the Declaration of Dawson Park or Servant's Last Stand which personally I think is a bad one because the only other guy I know who had a Last Stand was Custer and that didn't exactly go to plan. Anyway, if I was to tell you about everything I said in my speech I'd reduce you to an emotional wreck, so let me give you the main event which was the rabbit story.

I announced that I wanted to tell a story about a hare, a tortoise and a hamster. I started by talking about the hare running off up the road and the tortoise strolling off after it while the hamster just took it easy and watched them go. Once the other two had gone, the hamster bred like rabbits. I mentioned that I'd rather have used rabbits than hamsters in the story but rabbits were probably too close to hare, but the van owners shouted that they wouldn't have a problem with both hares and rabbits being in the story so I started again by talking about a hare, a tortoise and a rabbit. I talked about how the hare ran off up the road and the tortoise went strolling after him. The hare got so far in front he decided to have a kip right before the finish line and the tortoise caught up and strolled past the hare and the tortoise was nearly at the finish line when a shitload of rabbits all ran past him.

When I finished there was a stunned silence, like I knew there would be, and I closed my eyes and whispered 'Unite Or Die'. When I opened them people looked at me with a new level of respect and understanding. I nodded to Frank and he handed round the forms. These were membership forms for my Big Idea, a pressure group called Cheese Burger Van Owners (CHEBUVAO). I told the van owners that we needed to be organised and we needed to have a united front. Every time the media ran a story about the cheeseburger situation we needed a spokesman to be right there answering back with bells on. They asked who that spokesman should be and I scratched my left ear and Frank shouted 'Bob Servant' which may or may not have been connected to me scratching my ear.

There were a few grumbles about that but then I reminded them that I had a 'certain influence' over a 'certain committee' with a 'certain city council' and they caught my drift and agreed to my appointment. 'Just don't use that shit about the rabbits,' shouted one of them, which was a clever way of keeping me humble by pretending to make fun of me and I didn't have a problem with it.

At first I enjoyed being the spokesman of CHEBUVAO and the media mob liked me because I was a straight talker. Yes, some of my comments were maybe a little bit aggressive and some people say that by the end I was getting arrogant[67] but after two years in the job I'd become an absolute wreck. The original mania died down but, every week or two, someone would go into Ninewells with scurvy and it would all kick off again.

Not only was I dealing with the media, I was also having to keep Tuck, Gripper and Swapper on my side and that was becoming a big ask. They were under huge pressure and starting to crack. They banned Double Deckers, Two-Handed Burgers and Meat Attacks because they all had more calories than fifty Mars bars (as if that's a bad thing), but they were under constant pressure from the rest of the council and by August 1990 they were complaining that they felt like the Dutch boy with his cock[68] in the dam.

With all this on my shoulders I wasn't myself so when I got the invite to go on the TV show I said yes without thinking. All I was told was that it was a debate show, they admired my straight talking and they thought it should get a wider audience. It was on Grampian TV so Frank drove me up to Aberdeen in one of the vans then threw a major tantrum when I said he had to open up the van in the car park while I was inside doing the show. I told him business is like a shark, it never sleeps and you can lose a limb. Anyway, the debate was a complete stitch-up and the less said about it the better[69] but Frank did nearly thirty quid's worth while he was waiting.

---

67 See *The Dundee Courier*, various articles August 1988–August 1990 – ('Storm in a teacup . . . Piss off back to London . . . Cheeseburgers are healthier than bananas . . . Why don't you people go and chase proper criminals? . . . We're bigger than Jesus.)'.

68 Finger, presumably.

69 On 8 August 1990 Bob Servant appeared on Grampian Television's *North Tonight Special Report* entitled 'Cheese Burger or Cheese Murder?' I've got hold of the footage and it's spectacular. The other guests were a local doctor and a member of the Scottish Obesity Forum. The debate lasted just short of three minutes during which time Bob accused the Scottish Obesity Forum of being both Communists and 'perverts', accused the doctor of being 'knee deep in bungs from the Fish and Chips mob' and then angrily suggested that the show's presenter (who had yet to speak) was 'putting words in my mouth'. Bob walked off the set, only to reappear twenty seconds later to ask who he should speak to 'about expenses', at which point the show was replaced without warning by an old edition of *Sheepdog Trials*.

The fallout from the TV show, through no fault of mine, was pretty disastrous. The media said I was 'a madman' and that CHEBUVAO were acting like the mafia, former cheeseburger fans started abusing us in the street because of the Obesity Forum's lies, and my guys were booted off the council's Cheeseburger Van Licensing Committee and replaced by hardliners who came out in the press and said it was time the city's takeaway food scene went 'Back To Basics', which I didn't need a translator to know meant 'Fish and Chips'.

It was a complete overreaction, as if someone had pressed a switch marked Make Everyone Lose Their Marbles. I remember a few years later when Princess Diana died and there was a similar situation. I was watching the news with all the flowers and the hysteria and I shook my head and smiled sadly and said, 'Me and you, princess,' and Frank said, 'Me and you what?' and I had to give him a three-day ban from my house.

The end was in sight and a matter of weeks after the TV show cheeseburger vans were finally banned in Dundee. The Cheeseburgers Wars were over and like all good wars they ended with a party. Me and all the other van owners met at Broughty Ferry harbour, poured away the rest of our oil which made the most beautiful patterns on the water,[70] and then went by convoy to my house. Stewpot brought round a few kegs and things took off. It was a fantastic party with a great atmosphere and a lot of End Of An Era hugs and Best Days Of Our Lives back slaps. Late at night, with the music going and everyone dancing I looked round my house and realised two things. I was a King. But I was a King without a Palace.

---

70 See *The Scotsman* 4 September 1990 – '*Dundee RSPCA Investigating Swan "Armageddon"*. ("I wasn't in the Falklands," said passer-by Arthur Justice, 68, "but I'd imagine it looked exactly like this.")'.

30

Building the Anything Goes
Annexe to Bob's Palace

When I first bought the house that would become Bob's Palace it was already a very decent pad. It was nicer than Frank's for a start. Sometimes Frank and I will sit at mine and I'll say, 'Here, Frank, isn't it funny to think that even before I did all the work my house was nicer than yours?' and he'll kind of mutter and grumble and I'll say, 'Did you hear me OK, Frank? I was just saying that isn't it funny to think that even before I did all the work my house was nicer than yours?' and he'll sort of look straight ahead and start blinking really fast and I'll say, 'Sorry, Frank, I'm not sure if you're picking this up or not, I'm just saying that isn't it funny to think that even before I did all the work my house was nicer than yours?' and Frank will stand up and walk home really, really slowly.

When I bought the house it looked like this –

Bob's palace

These days it looks like this –

Old house

The Anything Goes Annexe

I know what you're doing. You're looking at the Anything Goes Annexe and it's up with your eyebrows. Well, I can't blame you and if you really knew what you were dealing with then you'd be peeling your eyebrows off the ceiling. Take your wildest dreams, mix in Sauce, sprinkle it with Excitement and then boil it in a saucepan marked No Rules while wearing an apron made of Danger. You're getting close.

The Anything Goes Annexe took a year and a good few quid to build (although I used pals so we didn't have to pay Kriss Akabusi)[71] but it was worth the wait because it's got the lot. Leather seats, a big telly, paintings of women on motorbikes, paintings of motorbikes on women, china dogs, wooden birds, mirrors in surprising places, doors in surprising places and a Hi-fi as powerful as a speedboat.

More important than any of that is the atmosphere. The Anything Goes Annexe has the best atmosphere of any room I've ever been in and that includes when the boy at the Eagle Bar put on Laughing Gas Mondays.[72] When I think of some of the scenes I've witnessed in the Anything Goes Annexe I find myself blushing. They're not

---

71 Sorry, problem with my 'replace all' function there.
72 See *The Dundee Courier,* Tuesday 18 March 1984 – *'Dundee Publican Fined.* ("He never told us," said furious Eagle Bar local Sid Berkeley, 36, "I had to go straight to my mother-in-law's cremation. It's shot my marriage to pieces.")'.

memories a Dundee man should have, they're the kind of things you'd expect to hear in anecdotes from George Best, Olly Reed or Forrest Whitaker.

The Annexe does strange things to people. Boys come round to mine and I walk them through the Old House and they're all 'nice cupboard' this and 'wonderful light in here' that and then they walk into the Anything Goes Annexe and their eyes go like saucers and it's all 'Where's the bar?' this and 'Tell the wife I've fallen down a manhole' that. I've seen good men, family men, pop round to tell me about a deal in Safeways and a few hours later they're sitting in their pants and talking about quitting their job to 'really give the acting thing a go'. I've seen one guy nip in for one drink and leave three days later having lost all his beliefs, though it wouldn't be fair to name him.[73]

Tommy Peanuts once came over and went home the next day with a black eye, reeking of perfume and with a woman's name and phone number written in lipstick on his back. It had only been me, him and Frank in the house but Sally Peanuts went bananas anyway. He was still allowed to come round but for a month wasn't allowed to enter the Annexe. One evening we were all having a party through there when I went back through to the Old House for some ice and clean socks. Tommy was sitting in a chair with his eyes closed and I thought he was asleep until he whispered 'Shoot me, Bob, just shoot me'.

Building the Anything Goes Annexe put yet another feather in my Being Famous In Dundee cap. It's been up and running for twenty years but to this day I still get nods and winks all over the city and I can see them nudge each other and say 'That's the Annexe, boy'. But it's not all beer and skittles because, to be fair, I've got as little control over what goes on in the Anything Goes Annexe today as I did twenty years ago.

Maybe you think that's unlikely. Well let me ask you this. If you lived next door to a lion for twenty years would you be confident about nipping round for a sandwich? If you lived with a shark in your bath for twenty years would you be confident about grabbing the backscratcher, throwing your towel off and giving it 'room for a small one'? No, of course you wouldn't. Some things can't be tamed and the Anything Goes Annexe is one of them.

---

73 See *Saving Father O'Neill from the vice-like grip of God and Jesus*

Here's an example. The other night Chappy, Frank, Slim Smith and Nervous Norrie came round for a game of cards in the Anything Goes Annexe. The cards never even came out the box. All I remember is Chappy being on all fours doing his German Shepherd material, Slim Smith lying on his side and shouting that he wasn't 'going to make it', Frank standing saluting with his trousers over his shoulders and Nervous Norrie getting trapped in the skylight. And that's a cards night. On a Tuesday.

So, yes, having the Anything Goes Annexe has won me some respect and recognition. But the lifestyle it's brought with it has cost me a hell of a lot in both time and industrial cleaning products. I'm not sure how many internationally respected Heroes spend Monday mornings wiping every sin imaginable from the walls and roof of their Annexe but I can't see it being more than a handful. You're probably looking at me and Hitler.

31

The Failure of Hands
Across The Water

Right, where are we? The nineties? Right, well, if we're talking nineties then we'd better start by talking Fife. In case you're not fully up to speed with the Dundee/Fife set-up here's a little map I've knocked up.

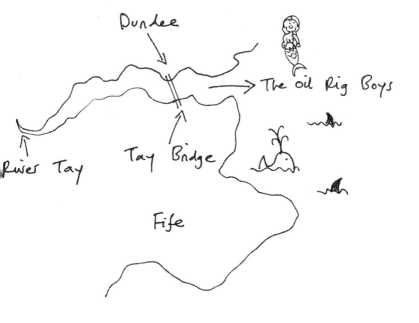

As you can see Dundee and Fife are either side of the River Tay. We're like two old friends sitting across a table and smiling at each other and saying 'How's Your Dinner?' while cars and trains go over bridges which I suppose would have to be on the table and sometimes a ship goes over the table on the way to the North Sea to see what it can do to help the oil rig boys.

It's only five minutes' drive over the Tay Bridge and with it being so close there's a lot of Dundee families who have seen members move over. There's always a lot of concern when it happens[74] but usually they manage to get messages across every few weeks and make sure that any children involved are still being taught the right traditions.

It's not Fife's fault that it's such a tough place. In the seventies and eighties the pits and the shipyards went and then in 1992 came the final-straw hammer blow with the sudden closure of the Dunfermline joke shop factory. That place employed 5,000 people and was the centre of the world's joke shop industry so when it went tits up things got critical.[75]

Every day there were more sob stories in the paper and it was hard for me to sit in my big house and look over the river and not feel bad for all those people. One morning I was sitting outside on my patio chair looking at Fife and something clicked in my head. It was as if Bob Geldof had got a train from London to Dundee, then a taxi to my house, paid the driver, sneaked round the back, crept up behind me, lay on his back, slid under the patio chair, poked his head between my legs, arched his back so his head suddenly appeared above my crotch and shouted 'For God's sake, Bob, do something!'

When you experience a moment like that, you don't piss about. I stood up, walked into my house, took a bit of paper and wrote four words – 'Hands Across The Water'. Hands Across The Water was one of the best ideas I ever had and, like Communism and the side parting,

---

74 See multiple stories in *The Dundee Courier*, for example 19 July 1985 – *'Police Can't Help Distraught Family* ("Under the current legislation we are unfortunately unable to consider their son's apparently forced relocation to Fife as a kidnapping," says a Tayside Police spokesman. "We understand their concerns, particularly on a safety level, but at the end of the day we have to consider the fact that he's thirty-two years of age.")'.

75 See *The Fife Herald*, 17 February 1992 – *'The Joke's Over For Fife* (Workers not laughing over factory switch to China . . . Environmental fears over "Sneezing Powder Mountain" . . . "I'm 53 years old and all I know is the correct voltage for a hand buzzer, what do I do now?")'.

just because it ultimately led to murder and famine that should not take away from how good an idea it originally was.

The first thing I did was nick a leaf out of Geldof's book and grab some celebrity endorsement. I took the Terry Wogan bucket out of retirement and wrote on it so it looked like Wogan was saying 'Do It For Fife!' That was me off and running. With the bucket in my hand, clever stuff going on in my brain and wearing a face that was serious but with a couple of touches involving my eyes to show I was still up for a joke if suitable, I walked with my head held extremely high into Stewpot's.

Now, I knew there would be a mixed response. Stewpot's has it's share of boo boys just like any other public institution, but I expected some decent stuff as well, such as smiles and nods, the odd cheer and maybe a rogue clap. And yes, if I'm being honest here, then I did wonder if the 'H' word would cross a few minds even if the people wouldn't have the confidence in themselves to actually say it.

Instead it was like I'd walked into an AGM of the Idiots, Boo Boys and Complete Bastards Club. Stewpot said he already had a window-cleaner (which was demeaning) and Frank went outside to do some breathing exercise which he said was unrelated but I'm fairly sure he'd seen the bucket and panicked about time travel. When I explained to the rest of the bar why I was there things got even worse. Tommy Peanuts said that this was what happened to men when they don't get enough skirt (which was demeaning and untrue) and Chappy started calling me Mother Theresa and tried to put a teatowel on my head.

I said that if everyone just threw a couple of quid in the bucket it would soon add up and I could go over there and help out the Fifers. The boo boys started up with stuff about me doing it for my own glory and how I should just hand over the money myself seeing as I was always banging on about being rich (which is total nonsense – I'll only admit to having a few quid if someone asks me, or looks like they want to ask me but are too nervous to do so).

I said I'd be willing to personally cover the majority of my expenses for the trip to Fife and, surprise surprise, that set them off again. Even when I said I'd only use donation money for basic stuff like drinks and maybe a set of golf clubs as a little 'thank you' to me for putting the whole thing together, they still didn't seem to get it. I told them it wasn't like Geldof had to buy his own fucking guitar for Live Aid but there's no point arguing with these people.

In the end I told them to forget the donations but that I was going over to Fife tomorrow to help them out anyway and then I played my trump card. The joke shop workers had staged a factory sit-in that had turned into a stand-off with the police[76] and so I gave it a bit of a shrug and 'But look lads, if you're scared you're scared, do you know what I mean?'

Smash, bang, wallop they were in my pocket. Stewpot shouted that we could take his Sierra, Chappy shouted he'd drive the Sierra if I bought lunch and Slim Smith shouted that he'd come if we didn't make any comments about how much he ate at lunch. I said, 'That's better,' and went outside to find Frank and tell him the plan. He said he'd come if I didn't bring up the time he tried to show the guy at the Tay Bridge tollbooth his passport and I told him the request was noted.

The next morning I got up early, made sandwiches for the trip and went to knock on Frank. He was a lot calmer than I thought he'd be but then told me he was wearing a wetsuit under his clothes in case he had to get back across the river if things kicked off. Unfortunately I didn't have time to make fun of him properly because Chappy beeped and we went outside and got in the Sierra where Slim was finishing off a pizza. I told him it was a bit early for a pizza but he said it was 'just a wee livener to get things going'.

The drive over the Tay Bridge was good fun. I brought up the time Frank tried to show the guy at the tollbooth his passport which raised the spirits of most people in the car and Slim polished off the sandwiches, which was annoying but also impressive, coming hot on the heels of the pizza.

We spent the morning driving around Fife. There were lots of Fifers about and only some of them had small faces like the boo boys say they do. We kept the windows up and the car was always moving but some of the Fifers looked not too different to us and when we waved at a few they just about managed to wave back. By lunchtime we were getting pretty hungry and, with things seeming relatively peaceful, we decided to risk a pub.

---

76 See *The Fife Herald*, 22 February 1992 – '*Police Surround Occupied Factory* ("We have intelligence that the main entrances have been defended with clusters of dog faeces and spiders," says a spokesman for Fife Police. "Although we believe that the vast majority of these items will in fact be plastic reproductions, there is always the risk that the saboteurs have taken a Russian Roulette approach.")'.

We found one in Tayport, not too far from the bridge, and Chappy parked up so the car was facing the road. We got out and went inside very, very slowly so they couldn't rush us. Slim asked to see the menu and I ordered a round of drinks and told Frank to get his wallet out. There was hardly anyone else in the pub so I relaxed a bit and told the barman we were over from Dundee and hoping to help out with the Fife situation. He looked a bit confused but didn't have time to answer because Frank leant over the bar and shouted at him 'I ONLY HAVE POUNDS WILL THAT BE OK, CHICO?'

I told Frank to take it easy and said to the barman that we'd read in the papers about all the hardship and were launching a charity drive in Dundee called Hands Across The Water. He asked what Hands Across The Water was all about and I was going to tell him when Slim said if he didn't eat something soon he'd pass out and Frank shouted 'DO YOU HAVE FOOD FOR US, AMIGO?' and acted out eating with his hands and mouth.

Chappy whispered, 'We're losing it here, Bob,' and I had to agree with him because the barman was starting to go a bit red. He asked what kind of help I was suggesting that Fife needed and I said that maybe Dundonians could boost Fifers' spirits by donating old clothes, or broken musical instruments or any sandwiches that they didn't particularly fancy. I don't know if it was my suggestion which made him snap or Frank asking if he'd like to be his penpal but things got very dangerous very quickly.

To this day I'm sure it was a metal bar that the barman pulled from under the counter. Chappy has always said it was a baseball bat, Frank suggested a sombrero and at the time Slim said big sausage but in hindsight he admitted that that his mind was playing tricks on him by that point and he'd already mistaken my head for a Christmas pudding.

We raced out the pub and got into the Sierra with seconds to spare. The barman chased us up the street but Chappy put his foot down and we Nigel Manselled it back over the bridge.

When you leave a place in that manner it's best not to go back and my relationship with Fife never really recovered. For months afterwards I'd sit in my garden looking at Fife and getting more and more angry. Hands Across The Water could have launched me into the Big League of famous charity Heroes but, because of the stubbornness of the Fifers, the whole shebang was cabbaged at the first hurdle.

1993 Broughty Ferry Harbour Day[77]

I'm man enough to admit that it all got a bit bigger in my head than it should have done, and things peaked at the 1993 Broughty Ferry Harbour Day. I was down there and everyone was admiring the boats and the demonstration from the Police Snorkelling Team but all I could see was Fife over the river and it felt like they were all laughing at me and winding me up and shouting unnecessary abuse about Hands Across The Water.

I took out a pen and wrote I'D RATHER BE A LIFER THAN A FIFER on my hanky and stormed the flagpole. The harbour master ran up there after me and managed to stop me getting my hanky up but I got a couple of good V-signs away. The paparazzi might have got me but I made my point and after that I felt ready to move on with my life.

---

77 Photo © *The Dundee Courier*, where it appeared alongside a 14 June 1993 article – '*Protester Only Blemish On "Best Ever" Harbour Day Party* ("I never thought I'd live to see snorkelling like that," said local man Arthur Justice, 71, "and I was in the Falklands".)'.

32

Saving Father O'Neill from the Vice-like Grip of God and Jesus

The first time I came into contact with Father O'Neill was during Tommy Peanuts' divorce. Sally Peanuts ran off with a guy from Maryfield who by all accounts had a Fiat Corsa and an unbeatable line in sarcasm and, almost definitely as a direct result, Tommy really lost the plot for a few months. We tried everything – 'forgetting' to make him buy his round, 'accidentally' telling stories that were based around New Beginnings, pointing out how much money he was going to save on groceries and shampoo. Nothing seemed to work and the next thing we'd heard he'd met some priest in Safeways and had decided to go to him for advice instead.

I wasn't particularly happy. Being subbied in favour of a priest for advice on skirt was a bitter pill to swallow but to my credit I bit my tongue and wished Tommy all the best. A few days later my patience was rewarded when he came into Stewpot's and said he was on the mend. Tommy reckoned this priest, who was called Father O'Neill, was 'one of the good guys' and that he didn't take Jesus or God too seriously and was willing to have a laugh at their expense.

I still wasn't too bowled over with the situation but the next night Tommy brought Father O'Neill into Stewpot's and the guy was a massive hit right from the start. Not only was he up for a laugh but he was more than happy to deal with the usual questions – does he pay for the communion wine, what's the funniest thing that the Pope's ever said to him and what's the nun situation? Then I asked where he lived and he said the church gives him a house and we just about fell off our stools.

I said that the only other jobs where you got a free house were a lighthouse keeper and the Prime Minister. Father O'Neill said that in one of those jobs you spent your days looking down at people and in the other job you were a lighthouse keeper. It was a clever joke, one of those ones where you say something like it's going to be one answer and at the very last moment you pull the rug away from everyone's feet and bring the house down. I appreciate a clever joke like that and although everyone was laughing I made it obvious with the way I looked at Father O'Neill that I completely understood the joke unlike certain others who were just laughing to be part of the crowd.

I went home that night feeling about ten feet tall. Fair enough, it was Tommy that had found Father O'Neill but he'd brought him into Stewpot's so as far as I was concerned he was fair game. I knew that if I could get Father O'Neill onside as a confirmed pal then all sorts of possibilities could open up for me. First though, I needed to get him away from the church. Being part of our gang takes a huge amount of commitment and if he was going to be involved then I had to free him from the vice-like grip of God and Jesus.

Getting people out of a religion isn't easy. There was the English long-jumper that gave up on God after punching that woman on *Songs of Praise*[78] but generally speaking it's hard for people to walk away because of the brainwashing. I decided that the only way I was going to free Father O'Neill was to use what must have coaxed him into the religious web in the first place. Words.

The next morning I tracked him down to the Jasper Carrott Soup Kitchen in Albany Road and asked if I could have a word with him. We went for a wee walk in Dawson Park and I softened things up with a story about skirt and Father O'Neill said that when it came to women he had a 'look but don't touch' policy and I told him Frank had been following that policy for years which made Father O'Neill crack up big time.

I waited until he'd finished laughing and then frowned as if this was all Off The Cuff and said, 'Here, Father O'Neill, this is probably

78 I think Bob is referring to the British triple-jumper Jonathan Edwards who regularly hosted teatime TV Christian favourite *Songs of Praise* until the 2007 news that he had lost his faith. Amidst a flurry of newspaper articles a friend of Edwards told the *Daily Mail* that the former athlete had suffered a 'spiritual meltdown'. The suggestion from Bob, however, that Edwards struck a female participant on *Songs of Praise* is entirely untrue.

bollocks but someone told me that Jesus has a massive nose like an ice-cream cone and great big feet like a clown. Anything in that?' Father O'Neill looked a bit shocked and said, 'No, someone's pulling your leg there, Bob.' 'Ah, OK,' I said and kept walking. I gave it a wee while and then asked, 'So you've met him then?' Father O'Neill said, 'Met who?' and I said, 'Jesus.' 'Jesus died two thousand years ago, Bob,' he said and I tried a 'Really? Two thousand years? Time flies, eh?' comeback.

I went back to the walking and looked around the park as if we were about to talk about the park and how nice it was and then BANG I went back with, 'So you've seen a photo of him then have you? Or a bit of video?' Father O'Neill was all over the shop by this point, he didn't know whether he was coming or going. 'Of who, Bob, Jesus? Of course I haven't,' he said. 'So how do you know he didn't look like that?' I asked and he said there were a few descriptions floating about and that I was being ridiculous. I held up my palms to say Just Relax and finished Stage One of my plan with, 'It would be hard to worship someone who had a nose like an ice-cream cone and big feet like a clown, that's all,' and he didn't say anything. That was the seed planted.

I suggested we went and had a go on the swings, which he didn't look too pleased about, but I said I just had a few more questions and that he could have first go. We went over and he sat down and I started pushing him which he enjoyed and once things were back to normal I told him I had a story to tell.

I told Father O'Neill that someone had told me about this guy called Trevor Turnips. I said that Trevor Turnips had apparently died a long time ago and no-one had ever seen a photo of him and no-one knew anyone who had actually met him, but there were rumours that Trevor Turnips was a really good guy and had done a few magic tricks and because of that some people were thinking of giving up their Sundays to go and sing songs about Trevor Turnips even though no-one really knew if Trevor Turnips was a real person or not and there was even the possibility that Trevor Turnips had a big nose like an ice-cream cone and great big feet like a clown. I asked Father O'Neill if he thought it made sense for me to become a fan of this Trevor Turnips guy because as far as I could see it looked like there were better things I could be doing.

Father O'Neill asked me to stop pushing him, got off the swing and walked away without a word. Later that night I was sitting in my house when there was a knock at my door. He came in and we went through to the Anything Goes Annexe. Three days later Father O'Neill left and the last I heard he was working as a taxi driver in Coupar Angus. I will never, ever reveal what happened in those three days other than to say there were a few scenes that I will take with me to the grave. Crying, screaming, curling up into a ball. And that was just Frank when I sent him in to clean up.

33

Accepting There's a Possibility That It's Just Me and Frank

I'll often turn on the telly or read the paper and there will be some article about how having sex can be tricky when you're older. I'll think to myself, 'Well you're spot-on there,' because over the last few years I've found it increasingly difficult to find someone to have sex with.

It's strange because if anything I've got more handsome as I've grown up. I was always a looker but I used to be a wee bit rough around the edges and now I've developed into one of those older men that you look at and your heart just melts, like Warren Beatty, Clint Eastwood and Eric Bristow. I've got the silver hair, the experienced walk and a whole range of smiles and looks that can do anything I want them to. My muscles are still there, you've just got to look a bit harder for them, and I've kept up to date with new fashions for clothes and swearwords.

So my problem with getting a bit of the good stuff isn't anything to do with me. It's all the fault of skirt levels, which are traditionally at their highest when you're in your twenties then begin to fall as skirt get picked off by other boys. From then it's a gradual decline apart from the occasional divorcee spike and a short-term boost after Hogmanay and April Fool's Day when there's a lot of trial separations going on.

By the time you get to my age, skirt levels are so low that available skirt should be made to wear flashing lights on their head. You end up looking for them and trying things out in unlikely places, and if I've been banned from Safeways once I've been banned a hundred times, but you just need to dust yourself down, apologise, put the baguette back on the shelf and move on.

Better to have the odd misunderstanding in a supermarket than end up trawling through your back catalogue, which I tried a few years ago with horrendous consequences. I started by phoning a few old flames and, to a man, they were a complete let-down. Sorry, to a woman. In fact I'd rather that they were men because at least then we could have got the saucy stuff out the way and had a wee chat about football or any belters that either of us had heard. Instead I had to listen to various excuses about marriages, families and the wish to forget a so-called 'moment of madness' up to forty years ago. I even went to a school reunion which was OK I suppose. I told a few stories from the old days and got a few people smiling and nodding but then it all got a bit confused at the end.[79]

My point is that you have to move on in life and for me that's becoming more and more about accepting that it might just be me and Frank until the game's up. Now, that would be depressing for anyone but for a man of my potential it cuts me to the quick because when I think about why I'm not a Hero to the punters I often wonder if it's the lack of regular skirt. Whenever you see these politicians on the telly, for example, they've always got skirt available to stand beside them in the garden when they admit to other skirt.

Ach, I've had plenty of adventures though. I could show you photos that would make you cry with pleasure and tell you stories that would make you want to do a Reggie Perrin on your family and move to Lochee. And I've not thrown the towel in completely. Hope springs eternal round my house, especially in the Annexe, and just this week I've put out a little feeler.[80]

---

79 See *The Dundee Courier*, 16 November 2005 – '*Man Ejected From School Reunion* ("They should have made it a lot clearer in their advertising that it was only for people who went to the school," says Servant, 59, of Broughty Ferry.)'.

80 I tracked down what Bob's referring to here. *The Dundee Courier* currently has a weekly section called *Lovestruck In Dundee* where people post sightings of others who have taken their fancy. I have included a selection, amongst which you might be able to spot Bob's.

Lovestruck in Dundee

You were on the 12 bus going to Douglas, with the wind in your hair. I was reading the Courier and wearing thick glasses. – *DT, Fintry*

You're in Mrs Muffins every morning buying a bacon roll, I'm the woman with the big chin who has extra brown sauce, do you have any sauce for me? – *RP, Monifieth*

I see you in the evening at the Brook Street bus stop. I'm the man in the brown suit. You're always on your phone. I wish you were talking to me. – *PB, Ardler*

I saw you loading your car at Safeways. You were struggling to work the brake on the trolley which is hardly rocket science. You had brown hair and it was all kind of jumbled up and you had a big yellow jumper on. You looked a bit like you'd been out and about the night before but that's OK, I like a woman that lets her hair down now and again as long as it doesn't get out of hand. If you start going out every night then you can chuck it as far as I'm concerned. – *BS, Broughty Ferry*

34

Not Becoming A Celebrity Even Though I Didn't Want To Be One Anyway Because I Hate That Stuff

My first book coming out was a wonderful time for me and those around me. That's not to say that there weren't a few hiccups along the way. One of the biggest hiccups was that, in hindsight, I probably started the build-up for the book coming out a little early. I'd been told that Word Of Mouth was the big one in building up interest so I started talking in Stewpot's about the book and the fact that I'd written a book around a year before publication.

After a week I was forced to wrap up the Word Of Mouth campaign when the Bitter and Twisted Brigade (led by, surprise surprise, Bitter and Twisted General Chappy Williams, Admiral Tommy Peanuts and Private Frank The Plank) reported me to Stewpot and he said I would be banned if I didn't stop 'blowing my own trumpet'. I told him that if that was blowing my own trumpet then whenever Chappy won a golf tournament we had to listen to a fucking brass band, but he said the decision had been made and that was that.

I was forced to keep my head down on the book front for nearly a year but when publication came round no-one could stop me talking about it because it got a belter of a review in Cruncher's magazine[81] and *The Courier* plastered me all over the front cover.[82] It's possible I got a little carried away in *The Courier* interview but it was an

---

81 See the Winter 2007 edition of *Mumblings From The Margins* ('. . . not without flaws but a charming bathroom companion.')
82 See the bottom right hand corner of page 37 of *The Dundee Courier*, 10 October 2007 – '*Broughty Man Says Book Can "Heal" City* ("This recession must be terrible for the normal punters out there and I hope that I'm putting a smile back on their credit crunched faces . . . I think my book will bring the city together and remind people that dreams do come true . . . More than anything I hope I'm an inspiration and I'm fairly confident that I am.")'.

exciting time for me because I was very confident the book would be the fuse to light a Hero cannon and fire me into Stardom Sky.

Not that I wanted to be a celebrity because I hate that stuff. Back in my day you'd turn on the telly or open a paper and you'd look at the people and you'd be thinking, 'Oh there he is again but he deserves it so good luck to the guy,' and 'She gets better every year and I must buy her new LP,' and so on. These were people you respected because of what they'd managed in life. They were brilliant actors, wonderful singers or genuinely world-class serial killers. Who do we get now? A bunch of no-marks and amateurs.

Unfortunately the coverage from Cruncher's magazine and *The Courier* didn't quite set off the clamour that I thought it would. A few days went by and then a few weeks and finally I had to face up to facts. As much as I hate that celebrity stuff it seems to be what the media want so I went to the newsagent and bought all the tabloids and the famous people magazines. One theme I noticed a lot of was secret photos of famous people who hadn't officially said they were shacked up along with articles giving it the Are They Or Aren't They routine.

That's what made me think of Lorraine Kelly. When she's not doing the telly stuff in London, Kelly lives in Dundee and I think she's married and so on but I thought that maybe the two of us could give the tabloids and famous people magazines 'something to play with'. I wrote her a letter suggesting a series of secret photos such as the two of us smiling and eating chips in Broughty Ferry harbour or walking along the beach holding hands or 'innocently' looking at the ring display at Simpson's Silver. Then I thought I could spot the photographer and he could get some shots of me giving the V-Sign and waving my hands and shouting 'Piss off!' and 'Give us some respect' and 'Go and chase real criminals'.

It was a plan that would have benefited us both (my book would have flown off the shelves and she'd have had more viewers than ever for *Countdown*) but I never heard back, which was tough but bearable because things had picked up in the meantime. Out the blue I'd had a call from Radio Tay who wanted me to go on Ally Bally's show which is big-time and, to be fair, I went down an absolute storm. [83]

83 My thanks to Radio Tay for supplying the tape of this show. Bob was the guest co-host on *Ally Bally's Afternoon Delight* on 23 October 2007. Amongst various

After the success of my radio appearance I decided I should make hay while the sun shines and put posters up at Stewpot's and Safeways that I thought would bring in a bit of business but, surprise surprise, the Dundee public lacked the confidence in themselves to pick up the phone.[84] After a few days of sitting looking at the phone and performing the sigh and shrug combination I thought, 'You're better than this, Bob,' stuck on my jacket and went for a Cheer Up For Christ's Sake walk along the Esplanade.

I was feeling a wee bit better when some boy cycled past and asked if I was the 'guy that wrote that book'. Straight away I felt about thirty feet tall. I said, 'Yep, you're spot-on there, pal,' and he said that he'd read it and then he said something else but it was quite windy and he was getting a bit further away and I shouted, 'What was that, mate?' and he tried again but he was pretty far away by that point so I started jogging and then I started running but he just kept cycling and then I was running like Linford Christie but he was cycling like Chris Hoy and it's no match when one boy's got a bike and he disappeared off up the Monifieth Road and I had to stop before I passed out.

As I stood there hunched over, spitting on the ground and my heart feeling like a football, I thought, 'Is this the Scottish big time? Does Billy Connolly chase boys on bikes along the road in America? Does Annie Lennox bomb it down streets in London because she thought she heard a whisper about her new LP? Does the boy from the Corries jog round the car park at Ben Nevis trying to get recognised? Because if this is the big time,' I thought to myself down at the Esplanade, 'you can keep it.'

(Then I just went home.)

---

highlights is Bob's dedicating of a record to 'anyone who was told that they were never going to achieve anything in life. If that turned out to be true, and you've not achieved anything in life, then I hope you at least enjoy this record.'
84 I recovered one of these posters from Bob's attic. I don't have much to say about it other than the fact that it's photographed overleaf.

35

Not Hearing Fuck All Back
on the Football Jobs

In December 2007 I was reading a story in the paper about how the Football Associations of Scotland, England and Ireland were all looking for new managers for their football team. I showed the reactions of a python and banged out letters to the three of them. Don't get me wrong, I didn't think I'd get the job but I thought I'd get a wee letter back and then I could stick them all up in Stewpot's and everyone would give it You're Some Boy and Have You Heard What He's Done Now. Knockabout humour always gets a good reception, just ask Jeremy Beadle or Prince Philip, but I never got the replies so, once again, I was let down by other people not being on my wavelength.[85]

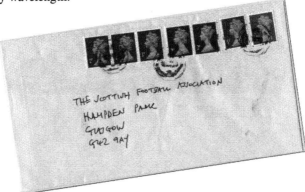

---

85 These following letters were indeed sent to the Football Associations of Scotland, England and Ireland in December 2007. Quite why they never responded I've got absolutely no idea.

Bob Servant
c/o Stewpot's Bar,
Broughty Ferry,
Dundee

Hello!

I am writing, as you have probably already worked out, to apply for the job of Scotland's national team manager. I see the last chap has buggered off down south and, well, fair play to him. I remember when Chappy Williams went to work in Perth for six months and a lot of people were having a right go at him, calling him a turncoat and a social climber, but what I always said is 'Come on lads, give him a chance, he's only doing it so he can buy a new Sierra'. Six months later Chappy was back in Stewpot's bar, buying the drinks and with a lovely Sierra parked up outside. So if the man McLeish wants to go and earn himself a Sierra, then I for one will not stand in his way.

You're probably wondering where you've heard my name before. Well if you have any Dundonians in the office walk up behind them in the canteen and whisper 'Bob Servant' and you just see what response you get. I have a hunch it will be a good one, put it that way. Or I think they'll know who I am, put it that way. In fact, sorry I don't know where the delete key is on a typewriter, put it this way I think they'll know who I am and they'll readily tell you that I'm a success story and let's not forget that success spreads like a disease. How will I spread my disease to the players? Easy, through my mouth. Five minutes before the players have to go out on the park and do their business I will ask for quiet and then hit them with this –

'Ok lads, here we go. This is the big one. Believe in yourselves because, as far as I'm concerned you're a bunch of crackers. Oh yes, you're a right mob of Bobby Dazzlers. Go on boys, go out there and do the business. Wipe the floor with those jokers, they couldn't lace your bloody boots. My God men, you're magnificent. I love you, you're like the sons I never had. Look after yourselves. And don't make the mistakes I've made over the years with the women. Don't be shallow and just go for the nice smile and the bazookas. Make sure they have decent walks as well. I've been involved with women with bad walks and it goes from being cute to being a major headache in a matter of hours. Imagine one of them coming up the aisle? All the boys nudging each other, having a laugh at your expense. The minister covering his face with the bible so you can't see that he's pissing himself as well. It's not worth it boys, take it from me because I've got the fucking t-shirt. Right, is everyone happy with their strips? We've got bigger shorts and socks if you need them. No? All OK? Great, well that's it then. Time to go. Action Jackson. William Wallace and Geronimo. Off you go you bunch of belters'.

Well, I imagine that's got your attention. You don't have to pay me a penny – all I want is one of those big jackets with my initials on it, but I would like my neighbour Frank to come in as right hand man and general dogsbody (that's general with a small 'g', don't give him a title). He says he needs to be paid enough to keep him in the lifestyle he's accustomed to so about five or six grand a year should do it.

Your Servant,

Bob Servant

THE Foots

Bob Servant
c/o Stewpot's Bar,
Broughty Ferry,
Dundee

Dear Sir,

I am writing, God help me, to apply for the England manager's job. Now, before I go on, I should hold my hands up and admit that I'm Scottish. I'm a Dundee man and I always have been and that's not up for negotiation. Don't give me the job and then put pressure on me to tell the press that I'm from Old Kent Road, Northumberland Avenue or Free Parking.

The other thing I should admit right from the off is that I've already applied for the Scotland job and, as far as I am aware, that is currently under serious consideration by the SFA. But don't for one minute think that I'm using you as a safety net. If I got offered both jobs then my neighbour Frank and I would be on the first train down to London (You'd have to have someone to meet us at the station though because we've only ever seen the place on *Bergerac*.).

But, like Gordon Brown and Lulu before me, I've got no problem with working with you people. Frank says he once met a couple from Birmingham in Aberdeen and they were perfectly OK and my friend Chappy Williams has a cousin in Swansea who's alright in small doses. Anyway, let's get on to the main question. What would I say to the boys before they go out? I'll tell you that right now. I'd wait until five minutes before kick-off, make sure they all had the right gear on and that it matched and then I'd say –

'Right boys, here we go. Now, listen up and listen good because I'm the gaffer here. Some of you are probably thinking "Where's the gaffer from? He doesn't talk like us". Well, I'll tell you. I'm from Dundee and Broughty Ferry to be precise, just down from Safeways. Some of you are probably thinking that it's not called Safeways anymore, that it's called Marks and Spencer's. I'm going to tell you two things. The first is that I will never call that shop anything other than Safeways until the day I die. And the second is that the game is about to start and we should really be talking tactics. So listen up. I want you to go out there and have some fun. I don't mean looking for skirt or telling each other belters. I mean having fun with the ball, passing it about and scoring wonderful goals. That's what the game's all about and that's what life's all about. OK boys off you. Not you Frank. Frank, why have you got a strip on? Captain?! Jesus Christ Frank! Sorry about this lads, off you go we'll see you out there. Right Frank, get that gear off and stick your tracksuit on. We'll talk about this later. You've whored this for us Frank, same old bloody story. I hope you're pleased with yourself'.

Well, what do you think? Send me your best offer. Let's not embarrass ourselves by haggling.

Your Servant,

Bob Servant

FooTRAY

Bob Servant
c/o Stewpot's Bar,
Broughty Ferry,
Dundee

Good Morning Ireland!

Well, here I am, Bob Servant, bravely reporting for duty to the Irish football team. First up, I'm not strictly Irish but I'm a Scottish Brother-In-Arms. I box out of Broughty Ferry, Dundee but if you gave me the job I'd be on a ferry before you could whisper 'Sinead O'Connor'. In fact that would be a fun way of telling me I had the job, I'll write my phone number on the envelope.

I've always felt close to Ireland, ever since I became a Wogan fan back in the 1970s and I include a photo of last year's Wogan birthday celebrations at Stewpot's bar. People talk about his laugh and his smile but my favourite bit of Wogan's body had always been those twinkly eyes that make him look like he's permanently up to something. I'm laughing now even thinking about them. What's he up to? What's Wogan up to now? Oh, God, I'm pissing myself here. The guy's a fucking lunatic.

Down to business. I want the Irish manager's job and I want it so badly I can't feel my feet. The full management team would be me, Bob Servant of Cheeseburger Wars and the Anything Goes Annex fame, and my neighbour Frank. He's been my right hand man since the burger vans and I'm not going to let him go now. Not when it looks like he's getting his cousin's car when she goes in for her hernia.

I know what you're thinking in the booming Irish voice in your head, you're thinking, 'It sounds good so far but what's Bob going to say to the boys before they run out?' Well, here's the thing. I'm not going to say anything, Frank is. I'm going to get all the boys standing in a circle with their strips on and their best boots and then I'm going to turn off the lights and climb up a stepladder. When I get to the top I'm going to turn on a torch and shine it directly down and say, very quietly, 'In you come Frank'.

Frank will come into the room in his green Incredible Hulk pyjamas (they're the closest we've got to a Leper Corn) and stand in the middle of the circle in the special torch spotlight. He'll be wearing sunglasses for the light and also to protect his dignity because at this point Frank will sing 'Danny Boy'.

About twenty years ago I was doing my business in the toilets at Stewpot's and I heard this sudden burst of 'Danny Boy'. I thought, aye, aye, Stewpot's got himself a new tape. I went out and said, 'When did you put the speakers in the toilet Stewpot?' He said, 'I've not Bob, have you been on the gin again?'

That was a cheap shot, I was well over the Gin Crisis by then, so I walked back through to the toilets with my head held high and was just in time to see Frank come out of the cubicle. I said 'Frank, you were magnificent in there', and he said 'I would hardly call it that Bob I'm having terrible problems', and I said 'No not that Frank, the singing' and he said 'Oh that, well it's always been a favourite'.

Since then we've made Frank bring out 'Danny Boy' on special occasions in Stewpot's and it never, ever fails to bring the house down. So when those players hear Frank sing I know for a fact it will make them feel about ten feet tall. Almost as tall as I'll be on the stepladder. When Frank finishes 'Danny Boy' I'm just going to turn off the torch so it's dark and say,

'I can't add to that, lads. On you go'.

And, once they find the door, I can guarantee that they'll run out and play like a bunch of Irish magicians. I look forward to hearing from you.

Your Servant,

Bob Servant

PS

I hope I got it right with the stamps. There was a bit of confusion in Stewpot's bar about how many I'd need for it to get to Ireland. Chappy Williams said half a dozen and Tommy Peanuts said you had to write AIR MAIL on it in red biro. Frank said he was told once that there was a special tunnel to Ireland that cats and dogs use but then Chappy Williams started laughing and said that it was him that had told Frank that and of course there's wasn't a tunnel and Frank shouted Oh I Suppose You Think You're Just The Funniest Man in Broughty Ferry Don't You Chappy and stormed out the pub. He'll be alright, don't worry, and will definitely have calmed down by the time we start work.

---

86 Luckily for my purposes, this application was returned to sender. Photo courtesy of Bob Servant's private collection, all rights reserved. Inscription on back of photograph reads: 'Wogan's 68th Birthday, 3 August 2006. I gave Frank a tenner.'

36

Dr Wilkie Stitching
Me Up Like a Kipper

When you get to my age there are loads of places you used to enjoy going to that you don't enjoy going anymore – places like Carnoustie, bouncy castles, and the toilet. The worst of all is going to the doctors. When I was a kid I used to love going to the doctor's because he had a big poster on his office wall of a naked woman. Well, I say that, it wasn't like a naked woman you get in jazz mags, it was more a drawing of a woman where you could see inside one half of her body and there were arrows pointing at her organs. But you could still see her outline OK and she had a nice eye.

The seventies were probably the golden age for going to the doctor. Back in those days there was a real 'anything goes' approach to comedy in doctors' waiting rooms and although I completely accept that some of that material doesn't have a place in today's society it was still enjoyable at the time. Unfortunately though, with regards to doctors, I suffered a Hiroshima in 1982 and the result was that I didn't go back for twenty years.

It was all the fault of a real snake in the grass called Dr Wilkie. He had just opened up in Queen Street and Chappy (golfer's shoulder) and Frank (questions about time travel) had both been to see him with separate issues. They raved about him and I'd been meaning to go and see him, so he could have the chance to meet me as much as vice versa, but hadn't got round to it when one day I was in Safeways giving the Small Ads Board the respect of a quick glance.

Amongst the usual Broken Hoovers and Unwanted Gifts Brigade there was a real diamond in the rough – a tiny little card that said 'Lovely Skirt', then a phone number, and then TWO kisses. I nearly dropped my basket. Safeways have a notoriously tough line on the content of the Small Ads Board (which I discovered when I was looking for a black pal) but they'd obviously missed this belter so I grabbed it, stuck it in my pocket and walked out in a Nothing Going On Here manner.

I got home and called the number. Some woman answered and put on this husky voice and did all that 'what time can you come round?' material and I thought here we go Bobby boy, here we bloody go. She lived in the Ferry, along in Long Lane, so I told her to give me twenty minutes and went to work. I had a bath, a shave, did my hair really nicely, went to town with the Cologne and stuck on my suit.

As I expected I got a bit of attention from the boo boys on my walk through the Ferry. A couple of kids said I smelt like their gran and I just gave it, 'Well that's a compliment to your gran,' then outside Toshy's Hardware some Know It All pointed out that my trousers were inside out. I got changed in someone's garden in Union Street and then walked down Long Lane with a decent smile on in case the woman was watching from a window.

I found her house and rang the bell then leant back on the gate so I looked like I was here, yes, but at the end of the day there were other places I could be as well. The door opened and she was not too bad at all and said, 'You must be here for the skirt?' I said, 'You could say that,' and did the Sean Connery trick of raising my right eyebrow. She said, 'Your wife's got good taste,' which was a pretty racy bit of flirting so I pushed myself off the gate, said, 'Luckily for you I'm not married,' and sent my left eyebrow up as well to show that things were escalating, even though sometimes when you send up both eyebrows it can be misread as surprise.

She was staring down at my crotch area and looking a bit rattled and I thought, 'Christ, we've got a live one here,' and I looked down to see that actually my trousers had been the right way round originally and the boo boy in Union Street hadn't been a Know It All but either short-sighted or a So-Called Comedian.

Before I had a chance to reply she produced a Safeways plastic bag and pulled out a tartan skirt and handed it to me. I was in shock. She told me I could have the skirt for free, she was just glad that it was going to a good home and closed the door in my face. I walked out the gate with my ears ringing with the terrible truth of the matter, turned round and, fuck my luck, Chappy and Frank were walking up the road. They were too close for me to leg it so I panicked, put the skirt over my head and gathered it around my neck.

They asked what I was up to and, thinking fast as always, I said I'd just been to see this Dr Wilkie they'd been banging on about and he'd given me a special scarf to stop me from getting the mumps. Obviously Frank swallowed it whole but Chappy looked a bit suspicious so I said Dr Wilkie had also suggested that draught beer could help so it was Drinks On Me at Stewpot's.

We got up there and although I got a few stares and Stewpot said something about not knowing I was so patriotic, I managed to move the conversation on. Things were going not too bad at all when I heard Chappy say, 'Hello Doctor Wilkie.' I couldn't believe my luck. I'd never seen the boy in my life and now slap, bang, wallop, he was in my pocket. I stared at the peanuts and then Chappy said, 'Bob was just telling us about the mumps scarf.' I spun on the stool and gave a decent one-two, saying, 'That's confidential, Chappy,' and then looking at the doctor in a very obvious 'help me out here mate' look. They obviously don't teach Basic Looks at Doctor College because the moron said, 'What's a mumps scarf?'

Chappy did a face that was exactly like a police dog catching the scent of a fugitive member of a prison chain gang in America's Deep South and pointed at the skirt. 'Bob here said that you'd given him this to wear round his neck to stop him catching mumps.' I tried one last look to the doctor, a pretty clear 'just go along with it' but the prick hit me with his own one-two. He said, 'I did no such thing,' then came over, looked for the label and announced, 'This is a woman's skirt.'

Chappy looked like he'd won the pools, he shouted for Stewpot to stop the music because he had an announcement to make. I wasn't going to give him the satisfaction of that so I stood up, pointed at Dr Wilkie and said with admirable politeness, 'You have behaved like Adolf Hitler today,' then walked out with my head held high though, to be fair, I could hear them laughing till I was two streets away, even through the thickness of the skirt. Things were pretty tricky for a wee while after that. Chappy told everyone that things had got worse and I'd started wearing high heels on my ears and Tommy Peanuts said that I'd had tiny pairs of tights made for my fingers.

Even after matters died down, Dr Wilkie's vindictive behaviour meant I didn't see a doctor for twenty years to demonstrate that I refused to be a whipping boy for their jokes. I had to go eventually when I had that thing with my belly button, and I'll pop in now and again these days, but I find it hard to drag myself along because they're such a bunch of drama queens. When you're sitting in a doctor's office and he's giving you the sad face and the Serious Lifestyle Issues routine just remember that about half of all doctors are failed actors and you'll suddenly understand why they're being so dramatic. Whenever one of them starts with the All Is Lost stuff I just smile patiently back and think that if they'd only got one cameo appearance in *Take The High Road*[87] then I wouldn't have to listen to this garbage.

I've got years ahead of me and I intend to enjoy them. But everyone dies once in their lives and on that front Bob Servant is no different to anyone else. Luckily, I've made arrangements. Not so luckily, they involve Frank.

---

87 A Scottish Television soap opera (1980–1993) famous in later years for eccentric scripting that saw characters' personalities alter significantly on an ongoing, day-to-day basis.

37

Not Trusting Frank With
My Funeral Masterplan

'Frank's in charge' is one of those phrases that just don't add up, like 'dry ski-slope' or 'well-known Aberdonian funny man' but with me being the last of the Broughty Ferry Servants I can't go down the normal funeral route of asking family to step up to the plate and start making phone calls once the Woe Is Me stuff is done.

I considered various pals to look after my Funeral Masterplan but in the end I realised that the most suitable person to be in charge was obvious. Me. So in order for me to be in charge I've told Frank that if I take the long walk into the sky before him (which would be a complete travesty for a start) then he's in charge. He got all excited and went down the It's An Honour and Won't Let You Down route and I just smiled to myself and thought, 'If you only knew,' because the fact of the matter is that I've given him so many rules that he's nothing but a puppet.

No Jokes

I know what funerals can be like. Everyone's in their best gear and the nerves start jangling and someone throws in a gag to break the ice. Well, not at mine because I want more ice than the North Pole with people concentrating on the job in hand and not rolling about in the aisles because Chappy's made some stupid joke. Me being dead is no laughing matter and people should respect that.

Lots of Crying

I watched this documentary once about a funeral in India. They light a big bonfire, chuck the dead person on it, then everyone sits about having a really good cry. In terms of the bonfire, I'd rather leave that to the professionals but I want to see some decent crying from the punters. Frank says that he can't see it happening because I know too many proud men and tough women but I tell him to remember about the music.

The Music

About ten years ago I was walking past Eastern Primary School when I heard a voice, stopped in my tracks and thought, 'Call off the search we've found an angel.' Despite the fact that it's got me into trouble in the past[88] I popped my head in the classroom window. The voice belonged to a little boy who was standing in front of the class singing 'Somewhere Over The Rainbow'. He had a funny wee face and little knobbly knees and my heart melted like chocolate. I drew up a contract on my hanky, waited until he came out for his break and right there and then signed him up to both my funeral and a management contract. He was eight years old and I was going to make him a star.

I gave up the making him a star bit after a knockback from Radio Tay and no reply from *Smash Hits* but I kept the funeral contract hanky safely filed away. A few months ago I was reviewing my Funeral Masterplan and decided to check up on my angel. I wish I'd never bothered.

Frank and I pushed the right questions into the right ears and we tracked down my angel to the fish and chip shop where he works. He doesn't work at one of the good ones like Maciocia's or Princess Friana's but at some chipper down near what was once briefly the Fatima Whitbread City Dump.[89] 'This doesn't look too clever, Bob,' said Frank when we got there and it was hard to disagree.

We went in to find this fat guy standing behind the counter. I asked him if he knew my angel and he went all funny and said it was him. 'You wish,' I said and then he pulled out his driving licence and I

---

88 See *The Dundee Courier* 23 June 1997 – '*Broughty Man Says He Was "Only Helping"* ("The children seemed unusually informed," said Mrs Blackburn, Head of Mathematics at Eastern Primary, "Until I overheard the gentleman whispering the answers from the window.")'.

89 See *The Dundee Courier*, 11 February 1990 – '*Arrogant English Athlete Refuses Council's Naming Honour*'.

had to swallow the bitter pill that my angel has grown into a donkey while Frank nearly ended himself with delight.

I told Frank to grow up and asked my angel what the hell had happened. He could see I was disappointed so insisted on loosening his apron and having a crack at 'Somewhere Over The Rainbow'. Fuck me, that was an experience. If the guy hit one note he did it by accident, Frank had to sit down because his legs went with the laughing and I thought I was going to die from embarrassment. I stared at the menu until he'd finished and then told him it was sad to see him like this, that he'd had the lot and thrown it all away and that I'd like a King Rib supper.

He said that was a bit much and how he's still only nineteen and I said that just made it even worse. It was a bit awkward after that because I had to wait ten minutes for my King Rib. Frank went out to the car to compose himself and I stared at my shoes. My so-called angel had a go at 'Wooly Bully' but I just raised a hand until he stopped. When I took the King Rib supper he was crying and I nearly cried too when I got home and tried to eat the thing.

Anyway, after that disaster I just thought, 'Keep it simple, no chances,' so I went and saw old Arthur Justice from the Broughty Ferry Amateur Dramatics Society. He agreed to put together what he called a Supergroup of the best singers from every Amateur Dramatics Society in Dundee. They're going to sing 'Holding Out For A Hero' while dressed as members of the Emergency Services and some of them will be bandaged up with tomato sauce on their heads so it looks like they've just come from a major accident. Good luck finding dry eyes when they get going.

Flowers

Arranged around the coffin I want to have those special flower letters like gangsters always have. On one side of the coffin I want flower letters saying HERO and on the other I want LEGEND. Frank says that people will think it's a gangster's funeral like when Fingers McConnachie died. That was the biggest funeral Dundee has ever seen because Fingers had everyone in his pocket including a certain newspaper editor. [90] I told Frank that people know I'm not a gangster

---

90 See *The Dundee Courier*, 18 March 1987 – '*Colourful Local Personality Passes Away*'. See *The Scotsman*, 18 March 1987 – '*Dundee Murderer Hacked To Death*'.

and that my funeral will be better than Fingers' because it won't have the element of fear or the inconvenience of the metal detector.

The Minister

Obviously Father O'Neill is out so it looks like I'll have to go with the Church of Scotland mob. One of the things I don't like about funerals is how the minister or priest makes it all about him and Jesus so I have told Frank to be very firm with the minister about this. I want him to concentrate on talking about me and to describe me as a Family Man because that always goes down well and gets the waterworks going amongst the punters. When we have our Funeral Masterplan Review Meetings Frank always gives me pelters for the Family Man line but I think it's fair enough. Every family I've ever met I've got on well with, sometimes very well, and as far as I'm concerned that makes me a Family Man.

Frank's Speech

I was kind enough to help Frank write his speech for the funeral. He grumbles about it a bit, saying that it's degrading to him and 'jazzes up' my situation but he's promised to have a go at it and I suppose that's all I can ask. Having said that, the material's so strong even Frank shouldn't be able to go too wrong.[91] After the joke ban, the crying, the music, the Family Man reference and Frank's speech, people are going to feel like they've been punched in the heart by Geoff Capes so it's only fair that they're allowed to let their hair down at the wake. Within reason.

The Wake

Frank has been told very clearly indeed that his job doesn't end when he leaves the church. He has two main duties at the wake. The first is to monitor the skirt situation. There will be some absolute crackers at my funeral, seriously top-drawer skirt. That's very much a compliment to me and it should be respected. The boys should

---

91 Frank let me see this speech, which was clearly typed out by Bob (complete with stage directions) and referred to by Frank as 'padded cell stuff'. It's on pp. 134–35.

stay away from the skirt at the wake unless they're going to talk to them about me and how sad it is that I'm not there to talk to the skirt myself and make them laugh like drains. Secondly any stories told about me, and God knows there will be a few, should be stories where I come out of the story well. If Chappy starts up with The Gin Crisis or any of my other temporary setbacks then Frank should set off the fire alarm.

The Funeral Critics

Dundee has some of the harshest funeral critics you'll ever meet but they're fair with it. Yes, they'll go to town with their reviews of a bad one but they recognise quality and effort when they see it and I hope to turn that to my advantage. I'd be surprised if anyone in the city has a better Funeral Masterplan in their funeral drawer than mine and that gives me a real opportunity. If this book doesn't make me a Hero, and I find that hard to believe, then I have to face the fact that I might arrive at my funeral as just another punter. If the Masterplan works out though, then I'll at least leave as a Hero. The weak link, of course, is Frank. But what can I do? I'm stuck with the situation. I'm stuck with Frank, I'm stuck with the fact I'm not far off needing a funeral and I'm stuck with the fact I live in Dundee.

Frank's Speech For Bob's
Funeral Which Was Written
Mostly By Frank

Good Afternoon Ladies and
Gentlemen, my name is Frank
and I was honoured to have
been considered a friend by
the late, great Robert Servant.
I would like to start by
thanking the minister for his
kind and accurate words and
also the Dramatic Society for
that fine rendition of Holding
Out For a Hero. It's funny
that they chose that song
because HERO is a word that
has been bouncing about my
otherwise empty head ever since
Bob was stolen from us. I know
from conversations with many of
you that you feel the same
way. I hear there have been
suggestions of some sort of
statue.

*If Chappy shouts 'from who?'
then just shout back 'From
too many people to mention and
casiy on*

Well, that's a discussion for
another day. But let me say
this. Words like HERO are
bandied about too much in
today's society. They should be
reserved for days like today
and men like Robert Servant.
Men wanted to be him, I know I
did. Women wanted to be with
him and I can see the
attraction. He had eyes like
Omar Sharif and a personality
that could be weighed by the
tonne. He's probably up there
now, sitting with Wogan and
laughing at us. Well Bob.

Look to roof

I hope you're having a good
time up there.

*— Do a thumbs
up to the roof*

I'll miss you Bob, if I can
call you that, and today's
record-breaking attendance
shows that I'm not alone.

Finally, I hope everyone here
can say that they gave Bob
Servant the right amount of
respect when he was alive, I
just hope that everyone here
can say that. Goodbye Bob.

*Stop and
look Chappy
in the eye*

Walk away, stop at the coffin and smile as if you
have just remembered one of my jokes and shake
your head as if to say — 'There will never be another
one like him, we have lost a legend here today'
and then walk back to your seat. When the coffin
starts to go into the fire let out a scream as if to
say 'Oh God! It's only just sinking in' and then cry.

When the people come out at the end and shake
your hand, say things like 'keep smiling', 'Be happy' and
'Bob wouldn't want to see you like this' and then cry.
To the top-class skirt say 'Bob always liked you' to
all of them separately. Tell the minister it was a
'decent' service, and whatever Stewpot charges for the
sandwiches, say 'You should be wearing a mask!' like
I do, and look at him as if to say, 'If only it
was Bob making the joke, not me' and then cry.

38

Liking Dundee Too Much

Well, here we are. Nearly done and the fat lady's about to swing.[92] I don't mind telling you that I'm bloody knackered. It's not easy this book lark. No wonder that bird from *Murder She Wrote* looks so old. I walk round the house and it's just paper, words and memories. But there's another smash book in those words and once again I've given it to the boy Forsyth on a plate – this house is getting like the Hit Factory – and then he swans in and does the interviews and I'm left wandering about Dundee looking for nods.

Telling your life story, the whole shebang, isn't easy. I feel like my brain has been pickled by a top chef and that my heart has been inflated with a foot pump by Russell Grant. But like a boxer on the ropes I'm pushing myself back into the ring for one last haymaker because I have a final thought on this Hero business and it's this – maybe the only possible reason left for me not to have become the undisputed Hero of Dundee is Dundee itself. Maybe I've been looking at things all wrong. If I didn't like Dundee so much then I could have been a Hero someplace else.

It's a scary thought, there's no doubt about that, but once it was in my head it took off like a pigeon. I started to realise all the things I could have done. I could have gone to Hollywood or Beverly Hills, whichever is closer, and stuck the black glasses on and smoked Hamlets round the swimming baths with the Big Shots.

I could have gone somewhere that my accent would have been seen as a novelty, like Australia or Greenland, and I could have gone to Africa and run about with my top off and had a laugh with the locals.

---

92 Sing, presumably.

I could have helped fly planes round the Bermuda Triangle, build pyramids in Egypt or cycle the Great Wall of China for a charity of Geldof's choosing as long as it wasn't one of those charities that make you dress up as a clown or a schoolgirl because I'd be taking the cycle itself seriously.

But, you know what? I'm glad I didn't do any of those things. I'm glad I stayed here. Because I don't think there's a harder place in the world to become a Hero than right here in Dundee, what with the boo boys and the weather. It's not Dundee's fault that I'm not the Hero Of Dundee. It's my fault for not telling my story sooner. From Mum, Dad and Uncle Harry to Alf Whicker and the Merchant Navy, to the Great Skirt Hunt and the window cleaning, to the Cheeseburger Wars to the Annexe to fifty years of Frank. If there's been a better story than that I've yet to read it and, yes, I'm including the Bible and *Where Eagles Dare*. Now that I've told it, things are going to change round here. You'll see.

Thanks for reading. Unless you're standing holding it in the shop, in which case you're an absolute disgrace.

Your Servant,

Bob Servant.

Acknowledgments

My thanks to – Hugh and all at Birlinn, David and all at MBA, Michael Munro, The Writers Room of New York City, The Dundee Rep Theatre, Jim Gove, Allan Reoch, Liam Brennan, Doc Ferry's Bar, the Taychreggan Hotel, Mark's Burger Bar on the Dryburgh Industrial Estate (great cheeseburgers), family, friends and all Bob's pals around the world. Now, most importantly, to Bob Servant.

On the day I left Bob's house, the manuscript tucked under my arm and a monolithic weight lifted from my shoulders, I found him waiting in his garden. He was sitting in one of a pair of deckchairs facing the River Tay, a generous glass of OVD rum clutched in his hand. Bob had been unusually melancholy since 'finishing the book' (as I have already described at embittered length in the Introduction, an optimistic phrase) and this final day was no exception. He patted the other deckchair and I sat down to a startling measure of rum and the question, 'Did I tell you about the day I finally sold my cheeseburger vans?'

This was interesting. I'd heard whispers of this fateful day from others and the general feeling was that Bob had in some way humiliated himself. I was therefore unsurprised by its omission from his memoirs and was too distraught from my existing labours to request it. And yet, with my departure minutes away, Bob began.

He told me that he had, through invite and bribery, gathered a crowd at Broughty Ferry harbour to hear an address where he would 'tell it like it is' in a wide-ranging speech that would have denigrated his perceived enemies in the council, local newspaper and the demonic Scottish Obesity Forum.

On the day itself, Bob related in a measured tone, such was the level of attendance that he elected to deliver the speech from the roof of his prize van. Frank was behind the wheel and the plan was that when Bob finished his triumphant talk, Frank would ease the van away and Bob would wave goodbye while holding onto the large plastic cheeseburger that crested his van and had become such an icon in the city.

'Frank, though, he . . .' Bob hesitated and shook his head with an ancient despair. 'I'd told him to drive me slowly the whole way home so I could wave to people and make it clear that it wasn't goodbye it was *buenos dias*.'

'*Au revoir*,' I prompted.

'No thanks,' said Bob, cryptically, before continuing.

Sipping at his OVD, the deckchair creaking as he braced himself for the story's climax, Bob told me that there had been a signalling mix-up between Frank and himself. Boldy predicting that the end of his speech would spark such an ovation Frank would be unable to hear instructions, Bob had taken with him to the roof a tube of salad cream. Frank's signal to start the engine was to be a quick squirt of the condiment onto the van's windscreen.

Bob hesitated in his deckchair. He seemed momentarily unsettled, as if locked in internal debate as to whether to tell me the story's end. His head hung a little when he continued, the words were drawn with regret.

'I'd only just started to speak, I hadn't even got to a joke,' he said, 'when a seagull shat on the glass and Frank went off like Jackie Stewart.'

From there, Bob told me, matters became unnaturally traumatic. He spoke of gripping the plastic cheeseburger in the appropriate belief that his life depended on it, of his bunnet being plucked from his head and his sheepskin coat being lifted like a cape into the air.[93]

'The Broughty Ferry Road was the worst,' he said. 'Like a wind tunnel. Then the Grey Street crossing nearly took my head off. When I got back here I had to put my arms in ice. I didn't speak for two days, who could blame me?'

The question, I think, was rhetorical and either way it provoked an extended silence. I, as is often the case, was left pondering blankly the motivation in telling me the story until Bob offered a sighed

---

93 See *The Dundee Courier*, 20 September 1990 – '*Tayside Police Clarify "Superman" Sightings*'.

clarification. 'That's what big goodbyes get you,' he said flatly, pointing at me. 'You see?'

'Yes,' I lied.

The roar of a toiling engine announced the arrival outside of Chappy Williams, Frank and Tommy Peanuts. Bob's three firmest companions had been at the local supermarket sourcing supplies for an evening's entertainment in the dramatic extension of Bob's house. They proceeded into the garden in fine spirits. Chappy, Bob's nemesis in a V-neck; Tommy, the Romantic lost to cycnicism; and Frank, the wide-eyed loyalist.

Frank looked at me in some alarm and exclaimed that there were 'only four chickens' but Bob calmed him with the assurance that I was 'on my way'. I obediently replaced my untouched drink, stood and said my farewells. Bob placed a warm hand on my shoulder which I took as a friendly touch before the force increased and I recognised it as more of a physical guide down his path. At the gate he said, 'Well done,' so quickly and quietly that I nearly missed it, before clearing his throat for all of our attention and declaring, 'Well, kiddo. Let me know if you're passing by.'

I reached for the gate and was pulling it open when he offered a final addition: 'So I can draw the curtains.'

Bob, Chappy and Tommy laughed with impressive abandon as I offered a stoic smile and walked into the street. For the final time I began the march along Harbour View Road. The sun was dipping into the Tay; its light lay on the water in great sweeps of orange. From behind me, I heard Frank start to laugh as well.

NF